Radical casework

Radical Casework
A Theory of Practice

Janis Fook

ALLEN&UNWIN

First published in 1993
Allen & Unwin Pty Ltd
83 Alexander St Crows Nest NSW 2065 Australia
Phone: (61 2) 8425 0100
Fax: (61 2) 9906 2218
E-mail: info@allenandunwin.com
Web: www.allenandunwin.com

National Library of Australia
Cataloguing-in-Publication entry:

Fook, Janis.
    Radical casework

    Bibliography.
    ISBN 1 86373 281 0

    1. Social case work. I. Title.

361.32

Set in 10/11pt Times by DOCUPRO, Sydney
Printed by SRM Production Services Sdn Bhd, Malaysia

15 14 13 12 11 10

Contents

CONTENTS

Tables

Acknowledgments

The ideas presented in this book have evolved over a number of years with the guidance and encouragement of several friends and colleagues.

I owe a special debt of gratitude to Allan Kellehear who has lived with me for the entire life of this project and has that true empathy, born of experience, towards the emotional and social toll that writing a book exacts. It was largely his wisdom and determination that sustained me.

Lindsey Napier and Sue Beecher will probably never fully appreciate their own contributions to this work. It was their belief in its importance, and their active use of it in teaching, which initially fuelled my efforts to record it in published form. I know I would never have attempted this book without their sincere and enthusiastic encouragement.

Ros Thorpe and Jude Petruchenia have consistently supported the work from the beginning through reading early drafts, and by publishing some of it in one of their edited volumes. Their advice and practical assistance have been invaluable to me.

Lastly thanks are due to the host of students and colleagues who have read and listened to my work, and have taken the trouble to pass on positive feedback, and to temper their negative judgements. I hope the book has done justice to the many pertinent questions they have raised.

Some sections of this work have been previously published in two separate books: *Gender Reclaimed*, eds H. Marchant and B. Wearing (1986) and *Social Change and Social Welfare Practice*, eds J. Petruchenia and R. Thorpe (1990); I wish to acknowledge and thank the publishers, Hale and Iremonger, Sydney, for this.

Introduction: Why radical casework?

Although the radical debate of the 1960s and 1970s transformed social work by introducing more political and collective forms of practice, the new perspectives had minimal effect on practice with individual people. As a social worker who trained in the 1970s, I found myself in my first job struggling to incorporate these new-found radical criticisms into my casework with people with disabilities and their families. Although it was technically a generic job, casework, especially co-work with psychologists, community nurses and psychiatrists, played a major role. Even the community development aspects still involved working with individuals and small groups of people who required sensitive interpersonal handling because of their long-standing experience of inadequate resources. Direct work with individuals, or casework of one form or another, still consumes much of the social worker's energy in the 1990s. It is therefore vital that we continue to develop our approaches to this work so that it is congruent with our broader levels of practice. As well, it is an ever-present challenge for professional social workers to convert their theory and analysis of people and society into workable principles upon which to take action. This book undertakes the double-edged challenge to draw up a framework of theoretical principles to guide the practice of a radical caseworker.

Many people have asked me why I persist in talking about *radical* casework rather than structural or socialist feminist perspectives. I like to identify this perspective as radical because I believe it is

1

RADICAL CASEWORK

important at the outset to see how casework practice can be directly informed by the critique and ensuing analysis which emerged from the radical debate of the 1960s and 1970s. It is a reminder too of some of the important reasons for radicalising and changing our practice. However, at the same time, it is equally important to recognise that more recent intellectual and social movements have also had profound impact on social work, in particular the feminist movement with its compelling analysis of the patriarchal system and its effects on personal lives. It is fitting therefore that if radical casework is to be a viable and meaningful approach in today's world, feminist analysis must be incorporated with earlier radical themes as a basis for social work practice in individual people's situations. The radical casework practice framework which is outlined in this book is therefore firmly grounded in socialist feminist theory.

Unfortunately there is still some debate about what radical social work actually is, yet we need to be clear about this before we can effectively apply the analysis to practice for ourselves. I have therefore organised the book in two parts. My aim in Part I is to clarify what radical social work is and to lay the theoretical foundation for a detailed model of radical casework practice. I will do this by identifying the elements of radical and traditional social work which can contribute to a model of radical casework practice. In chapter 1 I review the history of radical criticism and social work theories which have emerged subsequent to these. I conclude that a socialist feminist framework is the most suitable basis for radical practice. In chapter 2 I review potentially radical elements which need to be extended by socialist feminist theory to be truly radical.

In Part II I describe the detailed model, or theory of radical casework practice. I begin chapter 3 by describing the four fundamental elements of a theory of practice, and then outline the broad parameters of a radical casework theory of practice. Chapters 4 through 7 are detailed descriptions of each of the four aspects of this. The book ends with case illustrations and a discussion of further practical, ethical and theoretical issues, as well as an appendix of specific exercises and guides for the student and educator.

PART I

The theoretical basis of radical social casework

1 Radical social work

Radical social work as an idea and a form of practice has been widely discussed over the last three decades. It is an often maligned, and much misunderstood perspective in social work. There has been some doubt cast about whether or not to use it (Mowbray, 1981) or whether it is even meaningful to talk about such an approach (Smid & Van Krieken, 1984). Neither is there clear consensus on the nature of radical social work. However, I believe it is helpful to try to *clarify* our understanding, rather than simply avoid using the term, since the legacy of radical critique remains in post-modern forms of social work. I will begin by distilling the essence of radical debate from the last three decades.

RADICAL CRITICISM

Radical criticism first made a significant appearance in social work literature in the late 1960s, and therefore must be seen as linked with the social and political upheavals of that decade (Galper, 1980). Related intellectual movements, such as anti-psychiatry, the sociology of deviance (Walker & Beaumont, 1981), and sociological critiques of welfare approaches to poverty (Piven & Cloward, 1971) contributed to the development of radical social work criticism, and these beginnings from widely disparate sources partly account for its seemingly fragmented nature.

Some sociological critiques were directed at the entire base of the helpful professions (Mills, 1943; Halmos, 1965; Illich, 1970; North,

5

1972) for generating an ideology (system of ideas and related
practices) which perpetuated their dominant power over the groups
(of clients) they were ostensibly helping. Other critiques viewed the
whole social welfare institution (the social work profession
included) as an instrument of social control and, therefore, antithetical to clients' interests. Social work practices in general were
believed to inhibit social change (Pemberton & Locke, 1971; Galper,
1975), and indirectly contribute to the inherent oppression of the
existing capitalist system. The debate concentrated on social analysis
of social work and welfare institutions, and most of this was
Marxist-based (Skenridge & Lennie, 1978).

Critics from within the social work profession felt that there were
unresolvable dilemmas between the 'good' values of casework and
the 'bad' values of the society within which it was practised (Miller,
1968). Much criticism came to be directed *solely* at casework as the
main traditional form of social work practice, and debate raged in
the mid-1970s about whether casework was effective or not, whether
this could be tested, and if not, whether it was worthwhile continuing (Fischer, 1976). Others argued that the basically individualising
approach of casework 'blamed the victim' (Ryan, 1971) and therefore wrongly directed attention *away* from the society which caused
the problems. In this way, it was argued, individualised casework
help actually worked against individual people whose problems were
primarily structurally caused (Skenridge & Lennie, 1978).

Unfortunately, these criticisms were so broad that many social
workers felt it was almost impossible for any existing social work
practice to avoid them. Some felt the answer was to join unions and
political parties and work for social change through established
political channels outside the social work profession. Others concluded that since the criticisms were so nebulous, radical social work
hardly existed in practice (Clapton, 1977), and therefore need not
be taken seriously. Still others raised the argument that some
attempts to practice radical social work were not only inadequate,
they were really another form of conservative mystification (Considine, 1978), and implied that they should be avoided.

The clear challenge for radical social workers was therefore to
see whether or not it was possible to integrate broad radical analysis
with specific forms of radical social work practice. A number of
people attempted to do this from a number of different perspectives.
Corrigan and Leonard tried a Marxist approach (1978). A more
general socialist framework was preferred by others (Bolger et al.,
1981). The potential of the feminist movement to inform radical
practice was voiced by others (Dominelli & McLeod, 1982).
Another school talked about which values, philosophical approaches
and underlying assumptions would be relevant to an integrated

radical approach (Statham, 1978; London–Edinburgh Weekend Return Group, 1978). Other authors developed these ideas and refined them for their practical application (Bailey & Brake, 1978; Galper, 1980).

While little was written about radical social work in the decade of the 1980s, as feminist perspectives became more popular some radical literature began to reappear later in the decade (Marchant, 1986; Langan & Lee, 1989; Fook, 1990). From all this, common themes emerged to serve as a basis for radical social work theory.

COMMON THEMES OF RADICAL SOCIAL WORK

There are five main themes which are common in the radical social work literature:

- a structural analysis by which personal problems can be traced to causes in the socio-economic structure—therefore the individual 'victim' of these problematic social structures should not be 'blamed' for causing them;
- an ongoing analysis of the social control functions of the social work profession and the social welfare system;
- an ongoing critique of the existing social, political and economic arrangements;
- a commitment to protecting the individual person against oppression by more powerful individuals, groups or structures;
- goals of personal liberation and social change.

Structural analysis of personal problems

A radical perspective in social work first and foremost assumes an analysis which constantly links the causes of personal and social problems to problems in the socio-economic structure, rather than to inadequacies inherent in individual people or in socially disadvantaged minority groups. This analysis is the cornerstone of a radical approach, and is shared with socialist feminist approaches, which simply broaden the analysis by including the institution of gender as another problematic aspect of social structures. Problems as experienced by individual people are therefore not necessarily wholly explained by personal characteristics. A radical social worker always looks to socio-economic structures to determine what role they play in causing the problem situation.

Social control analysis of social work

Radical social workers should also be aware of how the social work profession, and the institution of social welfare of which it is only a part, function to control certain groups and individual members of those groups so that existing social and power divisions are maintained. This awareness should ensure that social workers do not unwittingly participate in activities which serve the interests of existing powerful groups to the detriment of the disadvantaged groups they are supposed to be assisting. This awareness of the potentially controlling functions of the social work profession should also indicate to the radical social worker ways in which controls can be minimised.

Critique of existing social arrangements

Not only do radical social workers need to be aware of how their own profession serves the interests of powerful groups, they need to be aware of how other institutions, groups and broader economic arrangements also do this. To put it more simply, radical social workers must be aware of the broad socio-political and economic context in which they themselves operate as individual workers and members of an established professional group, and how this context affects their day-to-day practice. They must be constantly aware of the possibility that these broader structures may influence their work and the situation of individual clients in ways which may be directly counterproductive to the interests of clients.

Protection of the individual person from oppression or exploitation

Armed with the foregoing critical awareness, the radical social worker is therefore committed to protecting the interests of individual people from oppression or exploitation by more powerful people, groups or structures. This anti-oppression stance translates into practice in many different ways. It may imply a stance which is anti-professional (for example, Laursen, 1975), or anti-middle class bias, anti-sexist or anti-cultural bias. In other cases it may mean protecting a person from a misuse of power or from overly bureaucratic and depersonalising structures and systems. The 'welfare rights' approach with its emphasis on advocacy (Terrell, 1973) is very much part of this tradition. Industrial deviancy and bureaucratic rule-bending (London–Edinburgh Weekend Return Group, 1978), or the 'bandit' approach to helping deviants (Means, 1979) are other variations.

Personal liberation and social change

Problematic social structures need to be changed if the welfare of individuals is to be achieved, and their effects counteracted in the lives of these individual people. Personal liberation and change is therefore inextricably linked to social change.

RECENT SOCIAL WORK THEORIES AND RADICAL SOCIAL WORK

How have social work theorists responded to these radical themes over the last two decades? Have there been any successful attempts to incorporate these into newer approaches to practice? The next section reviews these more recent theoretical developments to determine which aspects may be applicable to present-day radical social work.

Technical solutions

One of the easiest ways to apparently answer the claims of radical critics is to argue that there really isn't a great deal wrong with social work that a little improvement of its present state wouldn't fix. Simpkin (1982) calls these 'technical solutions'. People who support this view argue that social workers simply need to be more competent, more professional, or develop more exclusive social work knowledge, rather than to change any fundamental assumptions. Radicals of course would not entirely argue against this.

There certainly do need to be some technical improvements to the profession—we could do with being more competent, refining our social work knowledge, and in some cases increasing our professionalism, if that entails increasing the quality of our service to people who seek it. Radicals argue that there also needs to be a change in our fundamental understanding of ourselves as professionals and the way we view the causes of our clients' problems. The profession cannot be improved without this fundamental shift in understanding. Therefore any technical solutions which occur must be consistent with radical ideals.

Eclecticism

Another approach which has been proposed to address some of the radical criticism of social work is that of eclecticism. It is argued that since one of the problems of traditional casework is an over-reliance on the psychodynamic model (Fischer, 1976), one solution is to use a range of approaches instead (Chamberlain, 1975). Indeed, quite a number of new casework approaches (such as behaviour modification, family therapy, communication theory, crisis intervention, task-centred casework, role theory) has flooded the market in the last few decades (Cornwell, 1976), each emphasising aspects supposedly neglected by an exclusive psychodynamic framework. Caseworkers feel they are safe from criticism if they can pick and choose the appropriate approach for the appropriate problem.

There are of course some advantages with this course of action for the radical social worker. Certainly a broader range of explanations and interventions will maximise the potential for helping a person, and familiarity with a number of theoretical viewpoints will help to keep social workers critical of their own assumptions. On the other hand there are quite a few objections to an eclectic approach from a radical perspective. An eclectic approach is generally theoretically unsystematic which means that traditional 'blame the victim' ideologies can be just as easily utilised as a more structural analysis. Another drawback is the confusion and uncritical use of concepts which can result in social conformity. Too much piecemeal selection may so reduce the distinctive meaning and value of separate theories and disciplines that is all too easy to mould specific concepts into common wisdom. Unfortunately, this common wisdom is probably partly determined by the dominant social ideas of the particular place and time. In this way eclectic thinking may serve to bolster more conservative trends, rather than furthering critique of the existing state of affairs:

> Eclectic teaching all too frequently produces an apparent
> convergence of all disciplines towards one point of agreement: that
> of social convention. The theory is so reduced that the dynamic of
> the discipline is lost. There is often little distinction between
> theories which relate to social conscious and unconscious behaviour.
> Terms which are used in a specific psychoanalytic sense are
> broadened to take in common usage with all its accompanying
> confusion. (Statham, 1978:76)

This point underscores the importance of a clear and systematic base to guide the radical social worker's actions. The closer the integration of theory and practice, the greater the possibility of achieving radical aims.

Anti-psychiatry

The anti-psychiatry movement is included here because the ideas it put forward echoed and were reflected in the radical social work movement. The main tenet was an attack on the medical model or disease view of deviance, particularly mental illness (Pearson, 1975:15–17). Anti-psychiatrists argued against the definition of deviance as 'illness' and the resulting disenfranchising of the suffering person. Insanity was alternatively explained as a possibly sane reaction to an insane world. This thesis is important to radical social work for two reasons. First, it asserts the viability of the person's own perceptions of reality and thus questions the omniscience of the professional. If a radical caseworker affirms the person's subjective experience of that world, this may go some way towards guarding the individual from possible 'oppression' by professional structures, by overcoming professional distancing and authority structures (Davies, 1982:181). Secondly, it directs attention to the person's social environment as a cause of the problem, although again, as with systems theory, the exact links between the person's social environment and any actual experienced problem are not clearly spelt out.

Labelling and deviance theories

These are included because they add another dimension to the critique of the anti-psychiatrists. These theories attempt to explain the existence of social deviance through a particular social process— a type of social categorising which perpetuates and reinforces the behaviour in question. By society labelling deviants as belonging to a separate class, and thereby expecting and eliciting the requisite behaviour from them, the deviance is maintained. Recognition of the process, a sort of societal self-fulfilling prophecy, can explain many of the social problems encountered by social workers and is therefore a clear alternative to 'blaming the victim'. The society or people who label the deviant are blamed instead.

The labelling approach has obvious value to the radical caseworker, particularly because it stresses the need for non-stigmatising, non-punitive preventative welfare programs (Pearson, 1975:73). Where labelling and new deviance theories are of less value to the radical caseworker is in the extent to which they seek to provide an amoral analysis of deviance. The fact that all deviant groups are viewed with equal credibility means that, logically extended, there is no moral distinction between deviant and conventional. While it is essential not to pass value judgements on the lifestyles of those who are different from the mainstream, it is also essential to censure the hardship they may encounter as a result of their social differences, as well as the hardship they may cause to other groups or individuals. The amoral view is problematic because it tends to avoid a critique of conventional oppressive social arrangements, and indirectly helps to accommodate them (Gouldner in Pearson, 1975:72). This type of view would support a 'radical non-intervention' stance (Cohen, 1975), but in my view this is rather a cop-out. We need to know what we must do, not only what we must not, if we are to redress some of the very real wrongs of our current system.

Unitary or generic social work

The unitary, generic or integrated methods approach represents another attempt to reformulate the theoretical base of social work in the light of radical criticism. The main argument is that social work encompasses a variety of methods applied at different levels which are united by a core of common values and assumptions, such as self-determination and the concept of social functioning (Bartlett, 1970). The generic practice approach is therefore to confront problems in a professional manner to suit the level and method of intervention to the problem. Systems theory is a popular theory base for a generic approach (Pincus & Minahan, 1973). In a generic framework, methods of helping are often categorised as direct and indirect (Hepworth & Larsen, 1982), and casework is often referred to as 'interpersonal helping', implying that it is the interpersonal level of the generic social worker's repertoire.

For a radical social worker there are some advantages with a generic framework. It is important to remember that social workers may need to act on several levels with individual people, groups and communities, indirectly and directly, in order to bring about the desired outcome. It is also important to remember that no social work actions are or should be isolated, and that in order to bring about social change, radical social workers need to ensure that their actions as individual workers, whether oriented towards an individual case or towards society need to be linked with other collective efforts.

The main shortfall with a generic approach is its marked lack of explanatory content, in particular a class and conflict analysis (Armstrong & Gill, 1978). Although it is acknowledged that social work at all levels is linked and, if using a systems theory, that people are interconnected in systems, exactly how and why they are linked in particular ways is not adequately addressed. This means that as a guide to action, the generic approach is rather thin. Another problem of more serious concern to potential radical caseworkers is that the view of casework which is perpetrated by a generic approach is rather over-simplified and straitjacketed. The idea that casework is simply the direct or interpersonal level of generic social work omits the indirect work which a caseworker may need to perform with other people or systems within the person's situation in order to achieve the necessary change. The undue emphasis on interpersonal skills can also water down the dual social and psychological focus that casework is always supposed to have had, and thereby make a casework approach difficult to distinguish from some psychotherapies or counselling frameworks.

The ecological approach

Ecological approaches to social work practice represent an attempt to apply systems theory directly to the demands of social work. They have at their base an assumption that people can best be understood through the inter-relatedness of people and environment, and that what must be striven for is a 'goodness of fit' or adaption between people and their environment. Major exponents of this view are Germaine and Gitterman (1980) terming it the 'life' model. Their emphasis is on the potential for growth through these interactions. Stress comes about when the goodness of fit is upset.

For radical social workers this conception of people's problems has some currency, given that major importance is accorded to the person's relationship to the environment, rather than blame being solely directed towards the individual. The focus on interaction is also commendable, as this reaffirms the psycho-social nature of social work, and also indicates a clear point for intervention. Where the ecological approach falls short for the radical social worker is the failure to recognise the power differential between groups and individuals, so that it seems to be assumed that there is one common good to which all members of society are striving. It also ignores the institutional conditions which mitigate against adaptation (Naper & George, 1988). Therefore as a theoretical base for radical social work, ecological models are seriously lacking.

Marxist and socialist social work

These are probably the most popular theoretical approaches to which radically inclined social workers in the past subscribed. In general this literature relies heavily upon a socialist analysis, which initially was mainly in the form of critiques of the social control functions of social work and welfare. The Marxist concept of ideology was widely used to point up the specific ways in which the institution of social welfare upholds a system which works against the best interests of disadvantaged groups (Pemberton & Locke, 1971; Skenridge & Lennie, 1978). Later literature attempted to extend this analysis into paradigms for practice (for example, Corrigan & Leonard, 1978; Bailey & Brake, 1980; Galper, 1980).

For the bulk of these paradigms radical social work is one which adheres to the five themes outlined earlier in this chapter. However, there is a major emphasis on analysis, and rightly so. The argument that radical social work is as much, if not more, a change of attitude as of technique (Bailey & Brake, 1980:18–19; Simpkin, 1983:144) is certainly logically consistent with Marxist critique, since what much of the Marxist theory does is expose the ways in which social consciousness is formed and thus serves to sustain the existing social system. The first step necessary to overcome the social system is an awareness of how this happens. Leonard (1984) provides one of the few attempts to explain how social ideology actually forms individual personality.

Most Marxist or socialist social workers concentrated on the collective forms of possible action, such as community work, social and political action, and unionising (Corrigan & Leonard, 1978; Simpkin, 1983). There were some attempts to develop Freire's (1972) approach of conscientisation (Leonard, 1975; Keefe, 1980; Webb, 1985; Howe, 1987: 121–33) for use at individual level. Advocacy was also an early suggestion as an appropriate role for radical social workers (Terrell, 1973).

A major problem with Marxist or socialist perspectives was either their lack of application to practice, or the lack of a coherent set of practice principles. Specific techniques were taken up, and attempts made to make them relevant to social work (such as advocacy, conscientisation, welfare rights), but often without a view of how these were relevant to the aims of both the broad radical movement and social work.

Feminist perspectives

Feminist social work is one of the most recently developed approaches but it has caught and fired the imagination of so many social workers, women and men, that it has become well established in a very short space of time. The similarities between feminist analysis and radical analysis are now well documented (for example, Wilson, 1980), with the rider that feminist analysis actually extends a radical base by adding the crucial dimension of gender to any social critique (Marchant, 1986). There is already quite a plethora of feminist social work literature (Brook & Davis, 1985; Marchant & Wearing, 1986; Dominelli & McLeod, 1989).

Although feminism, like radicalism, incorporates a range of stances—liberal, socialist and radical (Bouchier, 1983)—there is a common core of theoretical analysis which deplores the way the patriarchal or sexist social structure systematically disadvantages women, and seeks to redress this disadvantage. In the early days, sex-role stereotyping (which was particularly enshrined in institutions such as the nuclear family) was seen as one of the major forms of this discrimination and, therefore, limiting sex roles and rigid nuclear family arrangements often came under attack. The analysis developed further, however, to try to redress the devaluing of traditional female characteristics (such as subjectivity, nurturance, non-competitiveness) which resulted from rigid stereotyping. Feminist analysis is also particularly successful at pointing up the direct links between social devaluation of women and their own self-deprecating beliefs. Feminists were also adamant that women's personal experience reflected the political context, and that in fact personal experience *is* political (Hanisch, 1971). In order to overcome these social limitations and enable personal liberation and social change, feminists realised that one of the major areas of necessary change was womens' beliefs about themselves and their social-political world. Therefore consciousness-raising, coupled with an ability to put these new awarenesses into practice, is an integral part of the feminist movement. This linking of analysis and action (praxis) is a cornerstone of feminist thought.

There are a number of obvious similarities between feminist perspectives and the earlier radical ideas. The need to constantly link theory and practice is one, but the analysis linking the personal experience to patriarchal social structures is just as important. The need for vigilant social critique is also implied, as are the goals of personal liberation and social change. In fact it is easy to argue that feminists have really taken up where radical critics left off. They have succeeded far better at connecting theory and practice, as well as the personal and the social. They have also provided many strategies for effective practice at both individual (for example, Fook, 1986) and collective levels.

Structural social work

Although not widely used in social work literature, 'structural social work' is the term used by some subscribers to principles similar to radical social work. In essence, structural perspectives refer to those approaches which place primacy on an analysis of social structures in understanding a person's situation (for example, Middleman & Goldberg, 1974; Moreau, 1979). Since this is one of the cornerstones of a radical approach, the two perspectives in this sense are one and the same. Structural perspectives can also subsume feminist ones, and in this sense the term is more general than 'radical'. However, because it is not widely used, and because I believe it is important to ground radical social work to the history and development of radical, and later feminist debate, I generally prefer to use the term 'radical'.

Discourse theory

This is probably the most recent theoretical development and is represented by the work of Rojek et al. (1988). It is based on the view that the ideas which people hold emerge from conversations and dialogues; that is, discourses between various groups in society (in this case social workers and clients). Rojek believes that it is valuable to analyse these 'received ideas' to achieve a more critical view of social workers, clients and problem situations. For radical social work, discourse theory may provide a valuable method of re-interpreting the ways in which the social environment determines ideas about client, problem and social worker interactions.

The major problem with such post-structural perspectives, however, is that they ignore the structural and material dimensions of people's experience. While radical social workers do need to deal with their own and clients' received ideas they also need to deal with the material, behavioural and structural aspects of societal restrictions.

The use of discourse theory may be a worthwhile direction for the future, once the clear parameters of radical social work practice are more firmly established. I find it more useful at this stage to deal with all aspects of ideology—the effects of 'mythological' beliefs and expectations on a person's behaviour, and how these support and are maintained by structural and material arrangements. The importance of this comprehensive focus is to provide a causal link between the individual person and the social structure, thus providing social workers with a strong and coherent theoretical base from which to understand personal problems. The beauty of the concept of ideology is that it also indicates clear points for action, so is ideal for indicating practice principles. To delve into the more complex domain of discourse theory is not the most pressing need for social work at the moment. Indeed, this newer, post-structural influence is still being developed in the discipline of sociology, and to include a detailed analysis of its influence here would, I believe, function to cloud rather than clarify the application of radical theory to direct practice.

A review of these recent theoretical developments shows that while there are some aspects of recent approaches which are highly applicable to radical social work, the wholesale adoption of solely one or another approach will not adequately address all five aspects of radical social work.

Another new trend which needs to be approached warily by supporters of a radical approach is the emphasis on specific concepts like empowerment (Furlong, 1987), social change, social justice and disadvantage (Chamberlain, 1988). Superficially, these concepts appear to be congruent with a radical approach but writers who use them do not necessarily draw on structural perspectives to inform their approach. Some are openly critical of the contribution of structural perspectives, particularly in casework practice (Furlong, 1987; Crawley, 1989). In this sense they do not contribute to the development of radical practice (Fook, 1987, 1989), since structural analysis is crucial to a radical approach. The clear need is to continue to link *all* aspects of radical analysis directly with practice.

FUTURE DIRECTIONS

Despite the attempts to integrate radical analysis with social work practice, many of the same problems persist, notably the lack of attention to practice models and strategies (Petruchenia & Thorpe, 1990:11), particularly at the individual level. Radical social work has not come very far on this dimension since early days of the critique (Langan & Lee, 1989:4). It is not sufficient to argue that radical social work is basically a change of analytical framework rather than technique. Since ideology also has practical aspects (Albury, 1976), a change in ideology should bring about a change in practices. It is this practical aspect of working with the psychological needs (Pearson, 1989) and personal situations of people with social problems which is really lacking in radical social work. Feminists had of course pointed out the ignorance of gender oppression by radical social workers and, more recently, the inattention to racial oppression has been noted (Langan & Lee, 1989:3). A particular problem noted by Australian social workers is the lack of locally developed and relevant material (Petruchenia & Thorpe, 1990:11; Healy, 1991).

Despite this and another criticism that radical social work is largely irrelevant to the Australian situation (Pemberton, 1982), the trenchant criticism from the 1960s and 1970s still rings true in many welfare settings of today. There is clear support gathering for the furtherance of such an approach (Langan & Lee, 1989; Healy, 1991). The journal *Australian Social Work* has recently called for papers on the topic (Fook, 1991) and given this renewed interest, it is important that the underdeveloped aspects of the 1970s radical social work be redressed. It would seem vital then that an up-to-date approach to radical practice must align itself with feminist social work, thereby combining an analysis of the institutions of class (as developed in a socialist approach) and gender in our understanding of people's experience. In this sense it is a socialist feminist approach (Wearing, 1986:47–52) which is most congruent with radical themes (Marchant, 1986). The clear challenge for radical social workers today is to develop a socialist feminist model for direct practice with individual people.

2   Can casework be radical?

Now that we are clear on the basic assumptions of radical theory, the next step is to try to develop a radical approach to the practice of social casework. The traditional concept of casework has received enormous criticism from radicals, but I believe it already has surprisingly much in common with the radical philosophies discussed in the last chapter. In comparing the common themes of the radical approach with traditional casework as it has been conceived over the past seventy years, it will become clear that at base, the ideals of traditional casework are similar to, albeit undeveloped, those of radical casework. One reason traditional casework has received such severe stricture may simply be because we have recently lost sight of the original dual (psycho-social) nature of casework. The result has been that we have relied unduly upon predominantly psychotherapeutic and counselling techniques with only minimal social emphasis. This may have led to an over-individualised view of personal problems and strategies for change.

STRUCTURAL ANALYSIS OF PERSONAL PROBLEMS

How much does the notion that the socio-economic structure causes personal problems figure in traditional conceptions of social casework? Historically, the social context of individual people's problems has been emphasised by caseworkers. In 1922, Mary Richmond (1922:98–9) described social casework as 'those processes which develop personality through adjustments consciously

19

effected, individual by individual, between men [*sic*] and their *social
environment*' [*emphasis added*]. Bowers (1949:417) characterised it
as an art which uses individual capacities and *community* resources
for better adjustment between clients and their *environment*. Later
Perlman (1957:4) referred to social casework as a 'process . . . to
help individuals cope more effectively with their problems in *social
functioning*' [*emphasis added*]. In the 1960s Brennan and Parker
(1966:16) stated that casework is aimed at helping the individual
solve problems in daily living, and more recently Gambrill (1983)
reaffirmed that awareness of social factors is assumed in a competent practice of casework. The concept that probably best summarises this dual (individual and social) nature of social casework is
Hamilton's 'person-in-situation' (in Mailick, 1977:407).

However, is this emphasis on the social context of problems the
same as an awareness of the structural reasons for personal difficulties? The answer hinges on what is meant by 'social context'. If
we look more closely at what earlier caseworkers meant by 'social',
it becomes clear they were referring to a person's immediate social
environment, or 'social milieu' as I like to term it. This embodies
a much more restricted idea of the way society influences individual
people, than does an awareness of the social structure extending to
include political, ideological and economic factors. It also involves
an underdeveloped confused analysis of interactions.

The social milieu of an individual (as invoked by traditional
theorists) embraces a totality of interactions which may occur with
other individuals in the family, groups or community in which the
person is a member (Wootton, 1959:287; Perlman, 1971a:31–2) and
while there have been varied attempts to describe these interactions
their precise *social* nature has not always been clearly spelt out.
This, of course, is not a shortcoming for which it is the sole
responsibility of the social work profession to redress. The exact
relationship between the individual and society has been a long-
standing dilemma for social theorists (Plant, 1970:1), and ultimately
it is to social theorists social workers must turn for the relationship
to be clearly described. However, whatever the reason for the
omission, the gap is a significant one for casework theorists, because
what appears to have happened in the absence of a detailed theory
of the relationship between individual and society is that *social*
interaction has been conceptualised as *interpersonal* interaction
rather than anything broader (Hamilton, 1951:22; Towle in Perlman,
1969:250). For the caseworker this can mean a narrowing of focus
and assistance. A caseworker concentrating on interpersonal interactions may focus on aspects of a person's communication patterns
in the workplace, or on how internal family norms might determine
self-identity. Using an analysis of the social structure and how it

influences individuals, the caseworker instead focuses on how the social institutions of work and family engender expectations of correct behaviour and attitudes towards other people (depending on their role and station in relation to each other). It is in this arena, of course, where the social theorists on whom radical critics rely, have much to offer. For example, the social relationships between individual people generally incorporate 'the historical and structural dimensions of role expectations' (Webb & Evans, 1978:22), like the sanctity of marriage, the proper roles for men and women, and the work ethic. As well, another dimension of the relationship is the influence that social and economic policies have on the material life opportunities of individuals.

Another consequence of confining the concept of social to inter-personal interactions is that there is still potential for 'blaming the victim'. In this case another individual is blamed, rather than the original person with the problem and blame is deflected from social structures.

In these senses, the social milieu concept of the social in tradi-tional social casework is not truly radical. It can divert attention away from the social structures which radical theorists argue cause and maintain individual problems, and may thus function to inhibit social change. However, the social milieu concept is at least one step towards radicalism, in that it attempts to explain individual problems through factors external to the individual. One of the challenges for a radical approach to casework then is to carry the notion of social further than 'family' or 'other people'. A radical approach to casework should focus on socio-economic factors such as class and power interests and associated ideological beliefs in meeting the individual problem. This, of course, entails two challenges: attaining a broadened focus, and attaining an ability to use this focus in casework practice. Let us look then at some aspects of casework practice.

The social history

The practice of taking a social history in order to collect relevant information for diagnosing casework strategies has long been advo-cated. Such information might include relationships with family, friends, employers; occupation; social status; membership of clubs; cultural background, and the like (Milford Conference, 1974:20–1). It was believed, reasonably enough, that collecting social informa-tion was the first step in tracing social causes of problems.

Unfortunately, such social histories tended to concentrate more on simply classifying the social aspects of individual cases, or on developing typologies of case categories (Mailick, 1977:404), rather than trying to determine any link between social factors and the personal manifestation of problems. The process was primarily descriptive rather than analytical. Thus, the radical principle of attributing socio-economic causes to individual problems has never really been fully developed in traditional casework because it has stopped short at the level of description rather than causation. A radical approach to casework then must extend the description to a detailed analysis of the relationship between individual and society such that causes of specific personal problems can be traced to particular aspects of the social structure.

There have been attempts to do this from a number of perspectives which are not radical: mainly the use of systems theory and the development of a generic theory base for all methods of social work. The problem with the broad generic approach is that it has tended to neglect the need to apply structural theory particularly in *casework* practice. It has been more concerned with developing methods which focus less on individual problems and have unwittingly so devalued the role of casework. With the generic approach casework has in many ways become reduced to the level of interpersonal helping, rather than appreciated as a truly psycho-social intervention (Fook, 1989a). If we are to develop a truly radical approach to casework practice then, we need to pick up where earlier work left off, and apply and develop specific theoretical links between aspects of the socio-economic structure and aspects of personal experiences.

Environmental modification

Traditional approaches see the main goal of casework as an adjustment between clients and their environment (Biestek, 1957:19). If adjustment in this sense is simply a conformity of the individual to society, this is obviously a non-radical stance (Rein, 1970:19–21). However, quite a deal of traditional casework literature implies that the adjustment is meant to cut both ways—that the person may need to adjust to fit the environment, but also that the environment may need to be modified to suit the needs of the individual. This is implied by the fact that although some primarily individually focused techniques are advocated (such as psychological support, insight, clarification), environmental techniques (such as 'environmental modification', 'mobilising resources') (Bowers, 1949:417) are also presented. Hollis (1950) discusses both categories of intervention. In a sense then, traditional approaches to casework have acknowledged the need to intervene in the environment and thus tacitly attributed some environmental responsibility for individual problems. For the radical critic, however, there are a number of marked limitations with this traditional approach.

First, 'environmental modification' has not really received near as much attention as interventions aimed at individual change (Perlman, 1971a). In 1969 it was noted that in direct practice, environmental manipulation had become peripheral. Social workers were becoming more sophisticated in the dynamics of interpersonal functioning (The Ad Hoc Committee on Advocacy, 1969:20). This trend has been echoed in many traditional casework textbooks where there is a dominance of psychological methods and techniques over social and environmental methods. Quite often the former occupy much larger portions of the books, and are more clearly identified and more specifically defined than sections dealing with 'social treatment' (see, for example, Hollis, 1964; Nursten, 1974; Hepworth & Larsen, 1982; Gambrill, 1983; Zastrow, 1985). In addition, case-work theorists themselves have noted the imbalance (Briar & Miller, 1971:4). Hollis, while agreeing that there is an under-emphasis on environmental factors, optimistically posited that this was limited to the 1940s and 1950s (1980:5–6). This may be true. However, an overview of casework literature prior to and including this period shows a faint equating of casework with psychological therapy, which became much more loudly debated during that time (Kasius, 1950). And there are remnants of this view expressed more recently. Take, for example, this quote from Briar and Miller (1971:4) that 'the distinction between casework and psychotherapy is merely professional', and the view that both may be categorised under systems of interpersonal helping expressed by Reid and Epstein (1972).

Some empirical evidence does bear this latter view out; for example, Fischer's studies of casework effectiveness (1976). As well, more recent British studies show that even though a variety of activities were and are practised as social casework (Stevenson & Parsloe, 1978), helping through interpersonal relationships, par-ticularly using a psychodynamic model, is either considered more prestigious than other more practical activities (Rees, 1978:54–5), or sharply differentiated from other activities as 'in depth' (as opposed to practical) work (Stevenson & Parsloe, 1978:105).

This higher value placed upon psychotherapeutic casework activ-ities (Irvine, 1966:38–46) may be both a result of and an explanation for traditional casework theorists' emphasis on such methods. In any case, despite the fact that traditional literature constantly asserts the dual psycho-social nature of casework in theory and practice, there appears to be an implicit preference for psychotherapeutic tech-niques, particularly in practice. I am not suggesting here that psy-chotherapeutic techniques must necessarily be non-social. As we will see later, much recent work has been done by feminists in particular to incorporate social explanation into psychologically therapeutic techniques. However, the bulk of psychotherapies upon which caseworkers have drawn traditionally have tended to rely on non-social or structural explanations of personality and behaviour.

A further major problem with the traditional conception of the dual nature of social casework is that although the primary focus of caseworkers is supposed to be on the *relationship* or *interaction between* the person and environment, in reality the focus may be on both separately. The result is frequently the adoption of separate strategies that only superficially alleviate the symptoms of the underlying problem. To illustrate, a caseworker dealing with personal and social aspects separately might deal with an unemployed person's depression through counselling, and with the unemployment through referral to an employment agency. However, if concentrating on the relationship between personal and social factors the caseworker might discuss with the person how his or her unemployment leads to feelings of depression, and conversely how these feelings make it more difficult to search for and obtain the work which suits.

It is important to draw this distinction between concentrating on the person–society relationship and concentrating on each element separately, because if dealt with separately, it is easy to see why psychological techniques might gain supremacy over environmental work. The clear and concrete development of psychotherapeutic, counselling and interpersonal skills makes them easier to teach and learn in both classroom and field situations, and the plethora of research, theory, manuals and laboratories surrounding them conveys an aura of scientific and academic respectability. Two points follow from this. First, that the social/environmental change strategies of casework require far greater attention, and secondly, that the truly interactional domain of casework needs to be reaffirmed. The first point will be addressed later in the book. Let us concentrate on the second point for the moment.

Interaction

Traditional views of casework indicate that the proper focus is the 'social functioning' of a person; that is, aspects of the person's psychological make-up or social environment which affect social functioning. However, as Coleman (1951:386) says, the main aim of social casework is 'to help the client with situational problems, not to modify character, attitudes or neurotic adaptations, although such may occur as a by-product'.

This can be extended to argue that the aim of social casework is to change people's social environment only in so far as it affects their relationship with it. This view is echoed by more recent social work authors who argue that the domain of social work is the point at which the individual and environment make direct and active contact (Rosenfeld, 1983; Martinez-Brawley, 1986). Conceivably this might include activities such as advocacy, but it would preclude larger scale environmental change (which was not primarily aimed at changing a particular person's situation) as the main aim of the caseworker. This is not to say that caseworkers should not attempt large-scale environmental change in a more generalist social work role. Nor should a caseworker practise in isolation from other social work activities. However, when practising strictly as a caseworker the focus should be on activities with direct and immediate bearing on the individual person's social situation. Thus the 'social' can be changed as it is manifested in the individual (for example, in the person's social expectations and beliefs, in the norms subscribed to, social pressures experienced, social ideologies that influence values and behaviour). Change that is focused on the person's social environment would involve, for example, re-interpreting the person's expectations and rights to other people in his or her life; 'rule-bending'; linking with resources; material aid, and so on as befits the particular situation. In this way we are reaffirming the *interactional* nature of casework while retaining the prime focus on individual help. In this way too there is a clear casework role (which is more than simply interpersonal help) within a broader social work approach.

For the radical then, this interpretation of the 'social' is already partially radical. However, this is more so in the explicit theoretical conceptions of casework from the literature, and less so in the implicit emphases on psychotherapy for intervention. Attention must shift to the interaction between the person and the social environment from the view of both as separate aspects which require separate attention. Clearer and more detailed links need to be made between the individual and social structure so that a coherent model for the practice of radical casework can emerge.

Individualisation: does it 'blame the victim'?

As we have seen, despite lip service to the psycho-social nature of casework, the focus of help has more often been the individual's situation. Is this individualised focus, or 'individualisation' as it is sometimes termed, the same as 'blaming the victim'?

As indicated in chapter 1, 'blaming the victim' is the course by which social problems are explained by reference to characteristics of the deviant group which has the problem (Ryan, 1971:8). For example, the existence of poverty might be explained by the lack of education, motivation, and low frustration tolerance levels or culture of poverty that poor people often exhibit. It is implied, therefore, that because poverty is a result of these characteristics, it may be combated by educating the poor, counselling them to improve their motivation, or subjecting them to behaviour modification to improve their frustration tolerance levels. In this way attention is diverted from socio-economic structures which have denied them education or employment opportunities. The 'victim' of the poverty is 'blamed' for its existence.

Looking more closely at the process, it becomes clear that no other cause but a causal relationship between the characteristics of the deviant group and their problem is posited. Moreover the causal link is one-way only: personal characteristics cause social problems, but not vice versa. Actions to alleviate the problem are directed solely at individual (or deviant group) change, not environmental or structural change.

If we examine traditional conceptions of social casework we see that this direct one-way cause of problems is not presumed. Historically caseworkers have been interested in social reform (Briar & Miller, 1971:4) and because of the long-standing psycho-social nature of casework, explanations for problems have been sought from a variety of disciplines. What casework has traditionally involved, however, is the focusing of intervention on the individual person (or on aspects of the immediate social environment).

Neither is this 'focusing' a cloak for 'blaming the victim'. To alleviate the victim's suffering caused by a particular situation is not the same as blaming that sufferer for causing that situation. It is perfectly possible to help the victim of a car accident and blame the other driver, road conditions, the weather, the state government, or God, for causing it. In addition, there may well be good reason (apart from clearly humanitarian ones) to concentrate assistance on the victim. These may be the only resources immediately available, and helping the victim does not necessarily preclude later bringing the other driver to justice, protesting about road conditions, voting against the government, or praying to God about the weather and Her or His injustice.

There are also other therapeutic reasons why it may be necessary and beneficial for radical caseworkers to alleviate the suffering of the individual victim. Sufferers may only become fully aware of the broader aspects of their condition once the immediate pain is allayed. They may also only perceive a *change* in that condition if and when their pain is diminished. It may therefore be necessary to treat the victim's suffering in order to bring about a change in the way their situation is perceived. In other words, we may need to individualise our intervention in order to stop victims blaming themselves.

Social casework can be accused of 'blaming the victim' if the

individual person, and only that person, is blamed for the problem.
If a caseworker, for example, only offers a poor person budget
counselling, fails to offer any other service (such as looking for
alternative sources of income), and attributes the person's continued
poverty to a failure to respond to counselling, then in effect that
person is being blamed for the poverty (both through the caseworker's analysis of the problem and choice of intervention). However,
if the caseworker provides material aid, encourages and provides
alternative opportunities, relieves the emotional symptoms of poverty (such as anxiety and depression), and acknowledges that social
difficulties may contribute to the person's poverty, then this caseworker is taking a potentially radical approach. The individual
victim is being helped to manage the particular social situation by
locating the causes for the problem in that person's social world.

Another aspect of individualisation that may be confused with
'blaming the victim' is the concept of 'individualisation' as an
accepted casework ethic—the traditional basic casework value of
respect for persons and a belief in their individual worth and dignity
(Biestek, 1957; Plant, 1970:8–12). While 'blaming the victim' is
essentially the assigning of a cause, the value of individualisation
is a professional ethic which assures that individual people are
treated as worthwhile. The latter is a *prescriptive* belief, the former,
descriptive. They are different orders of belief, and therefore cannot
be compared directly.

However, we can ask whether the ethical practice of individualisation may still lead to an ideology of 'blaming the victim'. Does
constantly recognising clients as individuals worthy of attention lead
inevitably to the conclusion that individuals are to blame for their
separate problems? Again, there appears to be no necessary link.
Just as feasibly, a caseworker may be led to the conclusion that
individuals undergo the same social experiences but see them differently. The caseworker's conclusion will depend on the theoretical
explanatory base they are using, not their moral or ethical base. In
other words, it is casework assumptions about causes of problems,
not beliefs about human rights, which are the crucial factors in
determining whether caseworkers blame the victim or not.

Yet another aspect of individualisation relevant to the caseworker
is the suiting of a 'solution' of the problem to the unique characteristics of the individual situation. As Brown (1966:11) says, 'Skill
in casework lies in the understanding of the different needs of
different people in various social circumstances and the provision
of different, appropriate kinds of help'. Individualisation in this
sense is the recognition that the same services are not necessarily
appropriate for the same cases. Casework has a mediating function
in ensuring a fit between an individual problem situation and the

services provided. Again, this is a potentially radical stance in that it can serve to ensure that personal needs are met, and the individual is not 'oppressed by the system'. Social casework has a history of looking broadly for the origins of problems, even if the links are poorly formulated. To further establish this radical potential and avoid blaming the victim, case-workers need to reaffirm this commitment to look for broad causes of problems. As well, the theory needs to be supported with practices which strengthen specific links between personal problems and social causes. In this sense, to be fully radical, caseworkers need to incorporate an element of 'blaming' the environment. Respecting the individual person and making sure casework help is appropriate to the specific situation are both congruent with radical ideals and should be maintained.

CASEWORK AND SOCIAL CONTROL

As is to be expected, social casework literature has been rather empty of well-developed sociological analyses of the profession and its controlling functions. In fact, few of these ideas appeared in any of the professions until the 1960s, as we discussed in chapter 1. Nevertheless, some less sophisticated notions of the 'social control' functions of social work, particularly casework, were current a decade earlier, mainly as an awareness of casework's responsibility to society; that is, to the social order which sanctions the activity (Lurie, 1954). Proponents of the functional approach to social casework showed marked acknowledgement of the bureaucratic con-text of their services (Hamilton, 1950:7–23) and later authors addressed the issue by drawing attention to the authority functions of social casework (Foren & Bailey, 1968). The potential conflict of these functions—that social work is caught between responsibility to the individual person and to society and the good of the one against the majority—has been continually noted (Perlman, 1971b:36).

These conceptions of social control, however, are only dim begin-nings of a radical analysis. Indeed, earlier critics, while recognising the potential conflict between the control functions of the profession and the commitment to individual welfare, thought that the dilemma could be resolved by the profession simply working towards the welfare of the entire society (Bruno, 1957:289). It is fair to say though, that although the full social control analysis is not developed into traditional conceptions of casework, at least the seeds of the dilemma it raises have been recognised. In a truly radical approach to casework practice, the full analysis of the profession's control functions needs to be incorporated into the ideological base from which workers operate, and specific strategies need to be developed which acknowledge or minimise these functions.

CRITIQUE OF EXISTING SOCIAL ARRANGEMENTS

Questioning the status quo should be a logical extension of the caseworker's traditional concern for the proper social functioning of the individual. If caseworkers are truly concerned about the social welfare of individual people, that should lead to questions about the adequacy of the existing social arrangements in fostering this welfare.

However, as with other radical tenets, the potential to question the status quo exists in theory, but whether it has meant anything in practice is another question. Casework activities which primarily attended to individual adjustment may have implied the necessity to question the adaptation of individual people, rather than the broader social surroundings.

Unfortunately casework literature does little to clarify this question. It is uncertain whether criticism of the existing state of affairs is seen as legitimate or not. Biestek asserts that 'the caseworker . . . is necessarily allied with the social, legal and moral good' (1957:94). Hamilton (1950:7–23) and Towle (1954:364) emphasise the inherent democracy of casework, which can only meaningfully be practised in a democratic society. The literature is bare of details about what constitutes the 'democratic good'. The writers may or may not assume that it exists in the present social system. However, as Plant (1971:51–70) has pointed out, while these are naive conceptions, they underline a moral dimension intrinsic in casework theory, and it is this moral aspect which may lay the basis for criticism of the present social order:

> It may be then, that in order to achieve their aim of developing the human personality through adjustment into social conditions the caseworker is necessarily led to formulate a critical theory of society in order to facilitate the fulfillment of the basic aims of the profession. (Plant, 1971:69–70)

The essential requirement then, is a critical theory of society. This aspect is underdeveloped in casework literature, yet it is one of the necessities continually raised for a theory of radical social work practice.

It is particularly important that a critical theory of society should include a realistic assessment of the limitations of professional social work power within present institutional systems. The radical caseworker needs to be aware of what avenues for action are possible within the existing structure, and what actions may be presently possible to change that structure. For example, radical caseworkers need to know to what extent they are bound by employment, bureaucratic, political, economic and even personal constraints. They may need to be aware of what professional and personal discretion can be exercised in given situations.

PROTECTING THE INDIVIDUAL

Social casework has a long-standing professional value base congruent with the ideal of protecting the individual from oppression or exploitation. In particular the traditional ethic of self-determination reflects a belief in individual autonomy: a recognition that clients have a right to self-direction and that caseworkers should respect and promote this. However, material and social limitations on this are acknowledged and some writers are quite definite that the right only exists within the present reality and social limitations (Biestek, 1957; Williams, 1982:27). This hardly amounts to a protection of individuals *against* the system—it is more a restrained protection of them *within* the system. Thus Plant (1971:37) says that social casework is really only committed to a weak theory of positive freedom; that is, a belief in the individual's capacity for rational self-direction and realisation. Nevertheless, as Webb (1981: 151) points out, such a commitment is still a wide step away from a conservative determinist model which minimises the person's potential to change her or his circumstances.

Keith-Lucas (1953:1076–91) argues that such a determinist tendency is more strongly allied with those casework approaches which rely heavily on psycho-analytic theory; that is, the 'diagnostic' school. By contrast, functional approaches, allowing greater scope for the exercise of individual free will, are ultimately more democratic. If this is the case, it is probable that the influx of humanist psychology and related existential therapies (such as client-centred therapies as in Cornwell, 1976) will increase the radical potential of caseworkers to protect individual clients from an oppressive environment, and to effect change upon it.

SOCIAL CHANGE AND PERSONAL LIBERATION

Social casework has long had goals of social reform (Plant, 1971:51–70; Mailick, 1977:403). However, as it is commonly argued (see, for example, Pritchard & Taylor, 1978) social *reform* is not necessarily the same as social *change*. The degree of the proposed change is the crucial element. There are basically two schools of thought on this issue: those who argue that change can only be wrought from within the existing capitalist structure (I shall call them liberal radicals) and those who work for 'revolutionary change by creating structures that presently do not exist' (Pritchard & Taylor, 1978), whom I shall call Marxist radicals. Although both have the same end in mind (a transformation of the existing system), they differ as to the kind of 'drasticness' of the strategies needed to bring about the required changes. Liberals advocate drastic reform, Marxists, drastic revolution. The differences between the two camps are ably illustrated by Pritchard and Taylor (1978) in their book-length debate on the two positions. Both perspectives are critical of each other. Marxists argue that a liberal approach is inadequate and largely ineffective because activities may be too piecemeal and therefore too open to reabsorption by conservative interests (Simpkin, 1979:138–9). Liberal proponents regard Marxists as providing too radical a challenge, one that is unrealistic given the activity of social work in its present form (Rolston & Smyth, 1982) and as developed from its particular historical origins (Webb, 1981:147).

While the 'reform or revolution' debate will never be fully resolved, it would be fair to say that a model for radical casework fits squarely into the liberal radical camp, as it is designed to transform a traditionally existing mode of practice within social work. I believe this type of approach to the practice of radical casework has potential to maximise the contribution of radical criticism by allowing immediate influence on present forms of practice.

The goal of personal liberation has not been entirely overlooked by traditional casework. There are some seeds of personal liberation in the long-standing ethic of self-determination, as discussed under 'Protecting the individual' preceding this. These are particularly reflected in some of the more recent moves of the 1970s to embrace humanistic, existential and client-centred models of psychotherapy, which place high value on personal responsibility. This is not quite the same as placing emphasis on personal power, but at least the ideas are not inconsistent. This aspect, however, does need further development if casework is to be more truly radical.

DIRECTIONS FOR RADICAL CASEWORK

Having examined the major traditions in casework theory, it appears quite convincingly that there is potential for radicalism within the existing traditional conceptions. There is a historical base of ideals and concepts which are essentially congruent with radical objectives which make casework potentially radical. However, this potential may have existed more in theory than in actual practice, and in some instances the theory may not have been developed enough to formulate clear guidelines for practice. Table 2.1 summarises the shortcomings we have discussed and the areas traditional casework needs to develop in order to realise its inherent radical potential. It also attempts to clearly differentiate these directions from the more conservative trends which also exist in traditional casework. Broadly in summary, the directions in which traditional casework needs to develop are:

1   Towards integrated *theory* of *practice* which links individual people with their socio-economic structure. If we are to develop a truly radical casework, we must concentrate on the *interplay* between individual and society in both our analysis of personal problems, and in the strategies we devise to act upon them. In particular this means we must both strengthen our analysis which illuminates the causal links between personal problems and social structure, and must ensure that the traditional 'social milieu' focus extends to a social structural understanding in practice. As well, one of the goals of casework is to place more emphasis on changing the person's situation and the way it's related to, rather than encouraging adjustment or conformity to the social environment.

2   Towards an awareness and acknowledgement of the ways casework can socially control clients. In handling personal troubles it is quite possible to direct blame away from the individual person and towards the social structure, while at the same time supporting the person's receptiveness to, and resources for change in the social structure. The long-standing ethics of self-determination and individual autonomy may be easily combined with a commitment to protecting individual rights in an oppressive, controlling society.

3   Towards ensuring casework is practised in conjunction with broader social work methods. To be practised more radically, the casework approach needs to contribute to social change efforts as much as possible, by joining with community or politically based actions. Casework should be viewed as one level (the individual) of generic social work practice. The understanding and information gained from practice at the individual level can provide unique and valuable insights into the social plight of many, and can directly contribute to efforts to change these situations.

Table 2.1 Identifying potentially radical elements of social casework

Non-radical	Radical
Conceptions of social factors are confined to social milieu	Conceptions of social factors are extended to social structure
Social factors are noted as background only, not used to explain problems	Social factors are noted and used to explain problems
Social factors are used only in analysis, not practice	Social factors are used in analysis *and* practice
Emphasises adjustment and conformity of the individual *to* the environment	Emphasises *changes between* the individual and the environment
Concentrates on psychological and/or social factors but does not link them	Concentrates on the interaction between psychological and social factors
'Blames' the individual as the sole cause of problems	Focuses on individual forms of help, respects the individual, blames the social structure
Uncritically naive acceptance of social control functions of social work	Well-developed critical analysis of social control functions of social work.
Uncritical acceptance of the status quo	Well-developed critical theory of society
Individual autonomy and rights protected *within* the system	Individual autonomy and rights *despite* the system
Inhibits social change	Contributes to social change
Casework is practised as the only, or isolated form of social work practice	Casework is practised as part of a broader form of social work practice

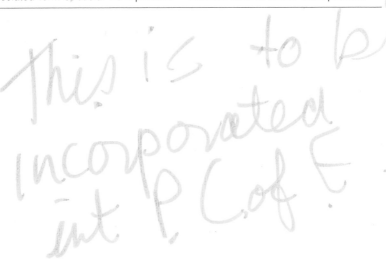

Radical social casework: a theory of practice

Introduction to Part II

So far we have established that a radical approach to casework is theoretically possible, but that to be truly radical the approach must adequately link personal problems with the social structure in *both* theory and practice. What has been lacking so far is a model which clearly does this in workable form. Radical social work literature to date has tended to concentrate on either explicating the critical analysis in great detail, or alternatively describing a set of practices without drawing their direct links with theoretical analysis of the situation. Both approaches are limited. As I have argued in Part I of this book, an over-concentration on theory will not necessarily achieve the desired social change. Neither will a focus on strategies necessarily achieve desired aims, because it may be too easy for these to be converted to non-radical ends. What is needed is a guiding framework which allows practitioners to constantly inform their practice with radical analysis and vice versa, as new situations are encountered. The framework is, therefore, neither *theory* nor *practice*. Rather it is a *theory of practice*—a set of guiding principles to link radical analysis with specific practice strategies. The emphasis is on integrating radical explanation into *all* aspects of the casework helping process.

It is a mistake to assume that 'practice' happens only at the end or interventive stage of the casework process. In fact we enact (or practice) our theory constantly, right through from the assumptions we make about the causes of people's problems, to the way we relate to them, the way we aim to help them and to the strategies we use to achieve these aims. The aim of Part II is, therefore, to describe this set of guiding principles in some detail.

Part II is organised by detailing each of the specific elements of this theory of practice. Chapter 3 begins by overviewing the theory of practice framework to show how each of the elements fit together. Chapters 4 to 7 detail the radical theory of practice model, discussing each of the five radical themes in turn, and illustrate these with case examples. Chapter 8 includes studies of six separate cases using a radical theory of practice framework. Chapter 9 concludes the book by discussing the more general issues and queries which have been raised about the context of radical casework practice.

3   A theory of practice

THEORIES OF PRACTICE

The need to integrate theory and practice is a major concern for all social workers whether traditional or radical. Unfortunately, there are long-standing problems in connecting the two (Lee, 1982; Barbour, 1984; Reay, 1986), which are sometimes viewed as completely separate and opposed to each other, as in 'theory versus practice' (Smid & Van Krieken, 1984). Of course radical social workers would ideally aim at 'praxis' or an ongoing reflective action. However, for the purposes of clarifying the thinking which is involved in translating theory into practice principles, I think it may be more useful at this stage to re-examine the common view that polarises theory and practice into only two separate domains. I propose we reconceptualise social work theorising and practices on three levels (Lee, 1982). Table 3.1 illustrates this. The first level incorporates the broad and unapplied theory and disciplines upon which social work draws (such as the social and behavioural sciences). The second level consists of the application of this theory to social work practice (such as theories of social work practice like the ecological approach). The third level consists of the actual practical strategies and skills which are used (for example, report writing, interviewing, interpersonal skills). This is informed by, and modifies the other two levels (Stevenson & Parsloe, 1978; Pemberton, 1981). Each level is as important as the other, and may occur simultaneously in relation to a specific situation.

Table 3.1 Social work theory and practice

		Examples
Level 1	Broad theory and knowledge base	Sociology, psychology, anthropology, social theory, philosophy, economics, etc.
Level 2	Theory of practice: general theoretical approach to practice	Social casework theory of practice: social factors, assessment, goals, methods
		Theories of therapy, e.g. crisis intervention, client-centred
		Theories of social work, e.g., problem-solving, ecological
		Approaches to community work, e.g. community development
Level 3	Specific practices	Report writing, agency procedures, interviewing, empathic listening, lobbying

It is the second 'middle' level which is the link between broad unapplied theories and specific practices, and this is the level upon which we need to focus. A theory of practice consists of the general guidelines which we use to help translate broad theoretical concepts so that specific practice strategies and techniques can be devised. Let us identify the components as described in most social work practice textbooks, in models for social work practice (Spitzer & Welsh, 1979; Schodek, 1981; Johnson, 1989; Compton & Galway, 1989), or in thinking about and planning casework action (for example, Roberts & Nee, 1970). These consist of:

1 concepts of human behaviour and personality, and of the individual's relationship to society (gleaned from first level broader theory and knowledge);

2 a framework for assessing the causes of problems in the person's situation (as deduced from the above);

3 formulating the goals of helping (as indicated by the causes of the problem and the ultimate goals of the broad theory);

4 formulating strategies for achieving the goals.

Table 3.2 helps to illustrate this model by applying it to traditional

casework and radical casework. The result in the first case is a
model that links personal problems with the limited social structure
and focuses goals on changing the individual. Applying the model
to radical casework as we have established it in chapters 1 and 2
shows the wider areas of concern that will be the domain of the
caseworker.

A DEFINITION OF THE RADICAL SOCIAL CASEWORK THEORY OF PRACTICE

Before we go into details of the theoretical model for radical
casework practice, it is important that we are clear on what radical
casework actually is, and how it differs from traditional casework.
Combining what we have already discussed about radical social
work, and the directions a radical caseworker needs to take, we can
in summary say that radical social casework is individually oriented
help which focuses on structural causes of personal problems, more
specifically on the interaction between the individual and the socio-
economic structure which causes problems. This structural analysis
is coupled with a critical approach to structures which control and
exploit individuals, and a commitment to protecting and liberating
individual people from these structures.

It is crucial that the radical caseworker is aware of the ways in
which the socio-economic structure influences individuals' lives, and
that this understanding is used in action. This understanding should
incorporate an explicit stance against inequitable or exploitative
social arrangements, and a commitment to exposing and changing
these where viable, so that the individual can gain more control in
life. The radical casework focus should be on aspects of the socio-
economic structure that impinge on the person; that is, social structural aspects of her or his life. Radical casework should free the
person from restrictive aspects of the social structure by providing,
for example, awareness about social role expectations, norms, pressures and ideology, that influence thoughts and behaviour. Change
that is focused on unique aspects of the social situation would
involve, for example, changing particular aspects which are brought
about by the social structure such as changing other people's restrictive expectations or behaviour, 'rule-bending', providing resources,
and so on, as befits the particular situation.

Table 3.2 explains the general theory of practice of such an
approach. The radical approach would emphasise the role of the
socio-economic structure on the person's situation. Casework problems are seen as caused primarily by inadequacies in this structure.
The aim is to change people's situations by establishing their control

Table 3.2 How a radical casework approach extends a traditional one

Theory of practice	Social dimension of traditional casework	Radical casework extension
Conceptions and social factors	'Social milieu' emphasis	Socio-economic structural emphasis
Assessment	Personal problems are caused by the person's inability to cope with her or his immediate social environment	Personal problems are caused by inadequacies in the socio-economic structure
Goals	To help the person adjust to and cope with her or his immediate social environment	To change the person's social situation by promoting her or his control over the effects of the socio-economic structure on their life
Methods	Strategies to help the person cope with her or his immediate social environment	Strategies to help the person change and control her or his social situation and structural aspects of her or his life

over the effects of this structure on their lives. Strategies to develop this control are devised. I will elaborate this model later in the chapter. At this point it might be useful to examine how this model of radical casework actually relates to a traditional model of casework.

THE RELATIONSHIP BETWEEN RADICAL AND TRADITIONAL CASEWORK

The major point of difference between radical and traditional casework lies in conceptions of the social environment. Traditional conceptions picture the social environment as mainly 'social milieu' or a conglomeration of interpersonal relationships and roles within the immediate social environment of family, friends and work colleagues. To become radical, the approach must be extended to incorporate notions of how the broader socio-economic structure such as dominant ideologies, power conflicts, and hidden exploitative or oppressive socio-economic practices and institutions affect individuals' lives. Thus, traditional casework can become radical if the 'social milieu' emphasis is extended to an emphasis on the (potentially exploitative aspects of the) socio-economic structure. Casework remains conservative if it is confined to analysis of, and action in the immediate 'social milieu' environment of the individual, or if the social situation is completely ignored, and only psychological factors noted and dealt with.

Radical social casework both *incorporates* potentially radical elements of traditional casework and *extends* these. First, it must incorporate some 'social milieu' aspects of the traditional view, since the influence of the socio-economic structure is often expressed in interpersonal relationships and roles performed in the person's immediate social surroundings. Thus, some traditional casework skills and conceptions used in dealing with the person's social milieu must be subsumed in a radical approach.

Secondly, a radical approach must also extend the purely psychological aspects of a traditional psycho-social approach. The links between personal psychology and social structure need to be recognised. So, while some aspects of psychological analysis and treatment may be useful, they must be balanced and weighed against structural explanations if the approach is to be truly radical.

Because the radical theory of practice I am proposing both incorporates and extends some elements of traditional casework, there is some overlap and similarity between the two approaches. Indeed, much radical casework practice may be little different from sound, traditional psycho-social practice, where the emphasis is on psycho-social interaction and enabling a better use of social resources.

While it is important that the radical casework theory of practice I am outlining should be integrated with all the traditional concepts and practices which have radical potential—including not just social intervention, but also psychologically oriented help which contributes to personal change and control—I will concentrate in this book on the *social* and *structural* dimensions of a radical approach, since these have been consistently underdeveloped in traditional approaches. I am not denying the existence of purely psychological or even material aspects of problems, nor the relevance of purely psychological or physical techniques to deal with them. However, I am arguing that a dimension of socio-economic and structural explanation always needs to be added, and that new strategies need to be devised, or old ones modified accordingly.

Table 3.2 illustrates how this radical approach incorporates and extends a traditional approach. Using the theory of practice outlined in the last section, the common aspects are easily compared. Thus a 'social milieu' emphasis is broadened to include the socio-economic structure in conceptualising social influences on individual lives. Personal problems, although possibly compounded by an inability to cope with the social environment, are primarily regarded as caused by inadequacies in the broader social structure.

Accordingly, the goal of radical casework is more far-reaching than that of traditional casework—to change people's social situation by promoting their control or power over the aspects of their lives which are affected by the social structure, rather than being limited to adjusting to, coping with or modifying their immediate environment. It may be necessary and relevant in a radical approach to limit some efforts to adjustment, coping and modifying, since some aspects of a person's existing social environment may be desirable and/or unchangeable. However, the ultimate radical goal is to *change* those aspects which are so desired. Similarly the methods of a radical caseworker will be geared towards promoting personal change and power, rather than limited to learning coping skills.

RADICAL SOCIAL CASEWORK: A THEORY OF PRACTICE

Let us look now at each of the components as they are used in a radical casework theory of practice.

The main aim of this section is to take the broadly labelled components of a radical theory of practice—the components of a theory of radical practice as we have identified them—and use them in actual case examples, thus demonstrating how practice according to the radical approach extends to the socio-economic structure from the point of the individual. The case strategies/examples are not meant to be comprehensive or prescriptive. They should be seen not as what necessarily should be done, but merely as examples using the radical theory and theory of practice so far established.

Table 3.3 serves to illustrate, using six examples, the difference between a traditional and a radical approach to how the social influences on personal lives are conceptualised.

The radical emphasis on socio-economic structure extends traditional limited notions of the immediate social environment. This does not mean that the social structure does not influence the

Table 3.3 Examples of social factors in traditional and radical casework

Traditional casework ('social milieu' emphasis)	Radical extension (socio-economic structural emphasis)
Communication patterns	Social power imbalances or inequalities
Role expectations	Dominant social ideological practices
Group or family norms	Dominant social ideological beliefs
Past social experiences	Historical and social change
Interpersonal relationships; social support networks	Social labelling processes
Material resources	Socio-economic structures

immediate social environment. A radical perspective in fact assumes such an influence, as is the case when socio-economic conditions affect housing and/or marital relationships. However, a radical approach also notes the structural influences on personal beliefs and behaviour, and how this in turn may serve to maintain existing social arrangements. For example, the acceptance of a social institution such as the nuclear family may mean that individual members hold beliefs in the sanctity of marriage, which in turn helps to preserve the nuclear family. There is therefore a direct relationship between individual consciousness and the social structure. In other words, the social structure is lived in individual experience (Leonard, 1984).

Let us take as a case example Jane, a 29-year-old mother, referred by the local school to a local community-based family welfare agency for assistance in managing her 6-year-old son Damian, who regularly refuses to attend school, often complaining of stomach pains, or sometimes simply refusing to leave the house. He occasionally throws tantrums and crying fits, which are highly distressing for Jane. Barry, Jane's 26-year-old husband and father of Damian, works as a truck driver and is regularly away from home for long periods. Damian's school difficulties are threatening Jane's new job as a receptionist, and Jane is concerned enough to seek professional assistance because her income is needed to meet rising mortgage repayments. Jane is also concerned about her marriage—she and Barry see little of each other, as he has had to increase his number of trips to try and increase his income. When he is home they often argue about Damian. Jane feels Barry spends too little time with him, and Barry claims that Jane is too soft with him.

Social factors

A traditional 'social milieu' perspective on this situation would concentrate on Jane and Damian's immediate environment for the causes of this problem, such as the family dynamics, relationships between Jane and Damian, Damian and Barry, Jane and Barry, other close family members; or problems at school or problems caused by work commitments. A radical approach would look at these factors, but also at broader social influences such as the social and financial demands on Jane and Barry as parents in a nuclear family, the relative social demands on Barry as father and Jane as mother, or the prevailing social expectations regarding schooling and normal behaviour.

In applying the six social factors set out in table 3.3 to Jane's situation, a traditional approach might focus on communication patterns in the home—how often Jane and Barry talk to each other, how often they all interact as a family. With a radical approach the worker might also look for any power inequalities within the family resulting from social beliefs about different roles within the family. Similarly, while a traditional approach might focus on role expectations within the family, a radical approach would extend this to look at the social reasons for family members adhering to them. A traditional worker might analyse Jane's situation by observing the dual social roles of disciplinarian and carer which she is expected to perform. A radical worker would acknowledge this, but carry the analysis further to realise how these dual expectations may function to blame Jane for the problem situation brought about by Damian's behaviour.

A traditional worker might observe the influence of the family's norms in the case: Barry may believe that Damian's behaviour is highly disgraceful, and reflects badly on his disciplinary ability, or that Damian is becoming too much of a 'mother's boy' because Jane is spoiling him. The radical worker would note these family norms, but would also look at whether these are a result of broader cultural or class norms. For example, Barry may feel that Damian's behaviour is a negative reflection on his own manhood, in that he is not asserting enough control over his family.

A traditional worker might then note the role of past social experiences in bringing about the present situation. For instance, Jane's present concern about Damian's behaviour might be linked to her own memories of being sent to school by her own mother. A radical worker might extend this vision to note how historical social changes have also led to school refusal behaviour becoming defined as more problematic, particularly with the increased tendency for women to work outside the home.

In a traditional approach, it is common to note the existence of interpersonal relationships and support networks. Whether Jane and Barry have friends or family who can assist with care of Damian is important. A radical worker, however, might also try to determine whether there is any social labelling or stigma attached by these other people to aspects of Jane and Barry's life, or Damian's behaviour. Perhaps Damian is seen as a 'behaviour problem' by the school, or Jane is labelled an 'inadequate mother' by some of the teachers.

Lastly, the adequacy of material resources is always an important factor. A traditional caseworker would be aware of how the family's financial circumstances and occupational requirements affect this situation. A more radical worker would look at how (or if) there are broader social conditions which bring this about, such as the lifestyle expected of truck drivers and their families, or inflexible work practices for working mothers.

Assessment

In casework, an assessment, or evaluation about the nature and cause of a problem, is made on the basis of information received about the social situation of a person. A traditional approach, you will recall, generally characterises problems as being caused by a person's inability to cope with, or adjust to, the social environment (Berlin & Kravetz, 1981; Northern, 1982). In some cases it may be acknowledged that there is a lack of facilities in their immediate environment. A radical view however extends this idea further to posit that the broader socio-economic structure may be at fault for not creating an environment which enables personal survival or social fulfilment. In the case of Jane, Barry and Damian, a traditional worker might characterise the general problem as being caused by Jane's inability to handle her son and help him adjust to being separated from her to attend school. A radical worker might recognise that although Damian's refusal to attend school and Jane's inability to deal with this are the presenting problems, they are the result of broader social conditions: legal requirements regarding school attendance, Jane and Barry's occupational and financial situation, and lack of alternative care options for Damian.

Table 3.4 takes the same social factors to the assessment stage illustrating some more specific ways in which traditional casework assessment may be expanded to more radical assessment. For example, if one of the social factors noted is the communication patterns between family members, a traditional worker might assess it is caused by inappropriate or ineffective communication. Thus Damian may be unwilling to go to school because of Jane's ambivalent messages about leaving him and going to work. He may be aware of his parents' disagreements over his discipline, and may be trying to test his mother's limits when his father is absent. A radical approach on the other hand, while recognising that Jane may feel ambivalent about leaving Damian, would also recognise that her ambivalence may be partly caused by general social expectations about motherhood, and Jane's relative powerlessness to juggle financial demands with the demands of motherhood.

A traditional view of the next factor may see problems caused by roles which are too stressful, unrealistic, or simply unable to be met. Jane and Barry may simply find it too difficult to cope with their chosen occupations and raising Damian as well. A radical worker would go one step further. Acknowledging the stresses of combining parenting and breadwinning roles, a radical caseworker may also locate some of the blame for the fact that people like Jane and Barry must persist in juggling both roles, on the existence of structural arrangements like the nuclear family. This dictates

Table 3.4 Examples of assessment in traditional and radical casework

Traditional casework: individuals cannot cope with their environment	Radical extension: the socio-economic structure is inadequate
Inappropriate or ineffective communication	Lack of power
Stressful role expectations; inability to fulfil roles; unrealistic role expectations	Ideological role restrictions: restrictive dominant social practices and beliefs
Conflict between group or family norms	Conflict of interest groups: hidden social functions of group norms
Negative learning from past social experience	Inability to personally change or cope with social change
Problematic interpersonal relationsips; lack of social support; social isolation	Effect of social labelling process
Lack of material resources	Prohibitive socio-economic structures

sometimes rigid role divisions which are impossible in straitened economic circumstances.

A traditional worker might conclude that one of the causes of the problem is simply a conflict of norms. For example, Barry may have been raised with different norms about schooling from those in Jane's family of origin. If Barry is from a working class background, and Jane from a more middle class upbringing, he may believe school is less important than she does. The problem is therefore caused by this clash of norms in which Damian is caught. A radical worker would not necessarily disagree with this as being part of the problem but might extend the analysis to look at how the different interests represented by this clash of norms both have controlling functions which add to the conflict in the situation. For example, if Damian does not attend school successfully, he is likely to remain working class in status. This would serve the interests of his father's class. If Damian does attend school successfully he will have conformed to the generally prevailing expectations regarding school education and is, therefore, more likely to succeed in approved channels. This may suit both his mother's and the prevailing social interests. The conflict therefore is not just about differences between Jane and Barry's family norms; it is also about the norms of different interest groups in society.

The fourth example posits that a traditional caseworker may assess a person's problem as being caused by past negative social experiences. For example, Jane may have experienced problems herself when attending school, which highlighted her own ambivalent relationship with her mother. A radical caseworker would not deny that this could be part of the problem. However she or he would also look further to any social changes which might add to the problem, such as the increased pressures on mothers to successfully combine family and work roles, and the ambivalence which results from this. The fifth example shows how a traditional worker might focus on problematic relationships or lack of social support as being a cause of the problem, but how a radical worker would extend this is to look at social reasons for this lack of support, such as the effect of social labelling. Although Jane's problem may be compounded because she has no one who can help her take Damian to school or mind him when he is unwell, the radical worker might also note whether the effect of Damian being labelled as a 'behaviour problem' makes it more difficult to find friends to help.

Finally, a traditional assessment that a person's problem is caused by a lack of material resources may be extended by a radical worker to note how prohibitive socio-economic structures can bring about this lack. In Jane and Barry's case inadequate finances are no doubt complicating their problem. A radical worker would also look at how schooling requirements, and the lack of flexible work and child care arrangements can make it exceptionally difficult for the two-income family to manage.

Goals

In general, traditional casework goals aim to help the person adjust to or cope with the existing social situation. Radical casework extends this to aim at helping the person actually change or control the existing social situation. Using our example case, the traditional worker might simply aim to help Jane and Damian adjust to the fact that Damian has to attend school, and Jane must work. A radical worker, however, might aim to help them change or control the situation in some way—perhaps the school situation may be modified in some way, or Jane's or Barry's work requirements made more flexible. The following examples look at these general goals in more detail.

Table 3.5 illustrates traditional and radical casework goals according to our same social factors. The first example illustrates how a traditional goal to improve communication can be extended by a radical worker to increase the power of any potentially exploited person in the situation. The traditional worker might aim to clarify messages between Jane and Damian, for example, and so reduce any ambivalence that has been communicated. The radical worker on the other hand might aim to ensure that Jane and Barry have equal decision-making rights about Damian's care, or that neither parent, or Damian himself, is unfairly blamed for the problem.

Table 3.5 Examples of goals in traditional and radical casework

Traditional casework: to help individuals adjust to and cope with their social situation	Radical extension: to help individuals change and control structural aspects of their social situation
Improve communication between individuals	Increase power of exploited persons
Relieve stress; modify expectations	Decrease ideological (both behavioural and belief) restrictions
Resolve conflict between individuals	Decrease exploitation by dominant interest groups; expose hidden social functions of group norms; equalise power imbalances
Unlearn negative associations; help separate present from past experiences	Increase ability to change and control life; awareness of the influence of broader historical and social change
Improve interpersonal relationships; increase social support	Withstand the effects of social labelling
Provide material resources	Provide material resources by changing prohibitive structures

Next, the traditional worker might aim to relieve the stress in the situation, or perhaps reduce the pressures of role expectations. Jane may be taught to accept her limitations, and not be overly worried if she can't be 'superwoman' juggling mothering and work roles. On the other hand a radical approach may aim to reduce the pressure of role expectations by actually decreasing role restrictions. For example, new role possibilities or choices about roles can be created. Jane may be shown how the mothering role need not be constant or all important or her sole responsibility. It may be acceptable to have 'time-out' from mothering and still be a good, or even better mother, and that enlisting the support of others is not a failure on her part.

The traditional casework goal to resolve conflict may actually extend, with a radical approach, to reduce any exploitation of less powerful people by the more powerful. This may be achieved by exposing any hidden interests being served by the situation, and which may actually be at the root of any visible conflict. In the case of Damian, Jane and Barry, a traditional casework aim might be to resolve the conflict between Barry and Jane regarding the discipline of Damian, by aiming to increase the agreement between the parents. A radical worker, while noting the conflict, might also aim to increase both Jane and Barry's sense of control in the situation, showing how both their different respective viewpoints about the importance of schooling can be linked to their own beliefs about what is Damian's rightful place. They could be encouraged therefore not to blame each other when trying to achieve what each believes to be socially acceptable for Damian.

In relation to the person's past experiences, and the possibility of change, the traditional worker may concentrate on helping the person 'unlearn' negative associations from past experiences, and to separate the present from the past; the radical worker should extend these to concentrate on making actual changes in that person's present life. Although it is important for Barry and Jane to see how their anxieties about schooling and discipline are related to possible deficiencies in their own upbringing, the radical worker would draw attention to the influence of present-day child-rearing expectations, and the range of Jane and Barry's choices in that context.

The next example focuses on how traditional goals of improving interpersonal and social relationships can be enhanced by increasing awareness of social labelling. For example, a traditional worker might aim to increase Jane's support from other parents. A radical worker, in working towards the same end, might try to further increase support to Jane by showing how her feelings of self-blame can come from the labels assigned by other people (such as school staff) believing she is a bad mother, and from the social labels she attracts in seeking professional assistance.

The final example shows how a traditional goal of providing material resources may be extended by a radical worker to change any structures which prohibit this. A traditional worker might recommend an after-school program for Damian which will allow Jane to make up some lost work time. A radical worker, perhaps discovering that Damian is ineligible for this because of his sometimes difficult behaviour at school, would then aim to challenge this policy, or to have his admission reconsidered on other grounds.

Strategies

Table 3.6 summarises how specific traditional methods can be extended in a radical way. Some of the terms used are new ones which I have coined myself in order to make the distinctions between traditional and more radical methods clearer. It is important to remember that some of the distinctions as set out in table 3.6 are not categorical; one radical strategy may be used to extend several more traditional practices. The role of advocate is an example of this, because it can be assumed in conjunction with many traditional methods. In other instances, it is more correct to view the difference between some traditional and more radical strategies as being on opposite ends of a continuum, rather than separated by a definite

RADICAL CASEWORK

Table 3.6 Examples of methods in traditional and radical casework

Traditional casework: strategies to enable personal adjustment and coping		Radical extension: strategies to enable personal change and control	
1	Skills, training; practical help	1	Social education
2	Passive use of resources	2	Active use of resources
3	Emotional empathy	3	Social empathy
4	Emotional support	4	Social support
5	Self-awareness counselling	5	Critical awareness; empowerment
6	Family therapy; relationship work	6	Advocacy

boundary. For example, skills training and social education can be seen in this way. Both involve teaching and learning, but the former is more behaviour-oriented, the latter more attitude-focused.

Example 1 in table 3.6 refers to skills training as a traditionally used strategy, and social education as a more radical technique. A traditional worker may teach people specific skills, such as decision making, problem solving, stress management, and social skills in order to help them cope with their situation. For example, a traditional worker may decide to teach Jane better communication skills to improve her relationship with Damian and Barry. A radical worker would recognise the necessity of learning specific skills, but would also emphasise the importance of changed thinking about these new skills. Therefore the emphasis is on changed *awareness* as well as changed *behaviour*, on *education* rather than mere *training*. From a radical point of view then, as well as learning better ways to communicate, it would also be important for Jane's family to think about why they should communicate in certain ways, and to begin to discriminate when certain ways of communicating will help achieve the desired result. This should also help them exercise more choice and control in their situation.

A similar point applies with example 2 regarding the use of material resources. Whereas a traditional worker may concentrate on providing resources, a more radical worker may also attempt to educate Jane and Barry about the process of receiving this assistance, so that they may seek it independently of the caseworker in future. For example, a traditional worker might give Jane the phone numbers of several different after-school programs. A radical worker might also help her work out how to approach the co-ordinators of each, and what to ask and do if Damian is refused admission.

Example 3 refers to how empathy can be used either in a traditional or a more radical way. A traditional use of empathy communicates the worker's understanding of how the person experiences the situation, usually with an emphasis on personal feelings. A radical approach would extend this empathy to also focus on the person's perceptions of both social world and experience. The traditional worker might empathise with Jane's feelings of frustration and isolation because of Barry's lack of understanding. The radical worker might pick up that she is feeling alone and frustrated because she thinks she is a social failure as a mother, and has no power in her situation.

The traditional concept of support can be extended in a similar way. Whereas a traditional worker may use emotional (and sometimes social) support to reassure people of their ability to cope in present circumstances, a more radical caseworker might also provide social support to encourage them to try new experiences; for example, a traditional worker might assure Jane that she is managing well under the circumstances and put her in touch with a parents' group to reinforce this. A radical worker might encourage Jane to gain support from people who are involved in new and different social activities from what is already familiar to her.

In example 5 the concept of counselling to provide self-awareness and to clarify or resolve conflicts can also be radically extended. A radical caseworker may extend people's awareness of internal needs and motivations to a critical awareness of social surroundings and their influence on those persons. This new awareness can also empower them to take more control in their life. For example, the traditional worker may counsel Jane to make her aware of her need to gain her own mother's approval in her mothering of Damian. A radical worker may concentrate on the social pressures Jane experiences to be a good mother.

Lastly, where a traditional worker might attempt to work as a therapist or counsellor in a professional relationship, a radical worker may take on an advocacy role in a more equal relationship with the person. Thus, instead of focusing on Jane's dysfunctional way of relating to Damian, a radical worker might act as her advocate in putting her view of the problem to Barry.

This chapter has illustrated how radical casework practice fits with (and basically extends) a more traditional casework practice. This was done by breaking down the model for practice into four components—social factors, assessment, goals and practical strategies, and then comparing traditional and radical aspects of each of these components by way of an illustrative case example (Jane, Barry and Damian). Now that we are clear on how the two approaches compare it is time to outline in much greater detail the actual model for radical casework practice. This will be done by taking each of the four elements of the theory of practice (social factors, assessment, goals and practice strategies) and dealing with each, chapter by chapter.

4   Social factors

In this chapter I will concentrate on extending the 'social milieu' conception of social factors used in traditional casework, to incorporate concepts of the socio-economic structure, thereby radicalising the theoretical base of casework. I do this by pinpointing specific working concepts which derive from radical theory (mainly in this case socialist feminist), and which clearly develop the nature of the relationship between the individual and the social structure.

SOCIO-ECONOMIC CAUSES OF PROBLEMS

The principle that problems are caused by socio-economic factors assumes a structural analysis of problems, so that the individual 'victim', or person in whose life the symptoms of the problems are manifested, is not blamed for causing them. This does not mean that individual people do not exacerbate their own problems through self-defeating behaviour (Goldberg, 1974:151). This point will be discussed in depth in the following chapter which discusses assessment. There we will look in more detail at identifying the extent to which structural factors determine individually experienced problems, and how particular interactions between personal and social factors may determine them. What we need to look at first, however, are those aspects of the social structure responsible for personal problems.

The concept of ideology

The first concept which is widely used by both feminist and socialist theorists is *ideology* (Wearing, 1985). It is invaluable to the radical caseworker because it clearly traces direct causal links between individual peoples' lives and the socio-economic structure. It shows how individual behaviours and perceptions are affected both materially and culturally by the system of inter-related ideas and institutions which is our social structure.

Ideology is a useful concept which shows how common social institutions such as work, the family, gender, class and ethnicity are supported by and also maintain individual thoughts and behaviour as well as a heirarchy of advantaged and disadvantaged groups within society. Let us discuss the concept in some detail.

The clearest definition of the concept I have seen is put forward by Albury (1976) who maintains that ideology refers to the totality of processes which form and maintain the social consciousness (or awareness or world view) held by the individual members of that society. In this sense ideology designates the social ways in which individual people perceive and experience their social world. We often speak of a dominant ideology—the body of beliefs which is held and maintained by most members of a given society, and functions to preserve the best interests of the group/s which is/are most powerful within that society. (Specific groups within a given society may also hold their own particular ideologies which function to maintain the identity and interests of that group.) It is possible to identify objective social processes which mould members' consciousness. They assume three forms: practical, theoretical and institutional.

The *practical* aspects of ideology are the patterns of social behaviour that express beliefs about social behaviour, and therefore become inculcated into the expected or normal behaviour of members of the particular society or group. Particular customs, rituals or roles are examples of this aspect of ideology. In social work for example, the practice of dressing to look like a professional person is a particular pattern of behaviour which reinforces the idea that there are differences between the social worker and clients (or non-professionals). A well-known gender-related example is the division of roles within the traditional nuclear family: women as child carers, men as breadwinners.

The *theoretical* aspect of ideology consists of the corresponding rationale and conceptualisations that arise from these practices. These serve to legitimise and explain the corresponding patterns of behaviour to private satisfaction, rather than explain the underlying ideology. As discussed in chapter 1, they include the 'myths', illusions and otherwise mistaken beliefs and assumptions that are held, not because they are necessarily true, but because they perform the function of preserving the dominant ideology (and therefore the interests of dominant groups). In social work, the practice of dressing to look like a professional person might be supported by the belief that looking like a professional will inspire the client's confidence and therefore aid in therapy. This may or may not be true. This is unimportant. What is important is that this belief justifies 'dressing like a professional' and also serves to preserve distinctions between professional and non-professional groups of people. An example of a gender-related belief is the idea that men are genetically better suited to the rigours of earning money outside the domestic home, and women to more sensitive child care duties.

The *institutional* aspect of ideology is that which is responsible for the maintenance, production and reproduction of these specific ideas. It ensures that individual members of society take on the habits, attitudes and conceptions which are appropriate to their society. It is also the level at which the theoretical and practical aspects (or beliefs and behaviours) are organised into systems of inter-related assumptions and practices. Examples of social institutions include the family, education, work, social class, gender and culture. In social work, an example of the institutional aspect of ideology might be all the processes needed to ensure that social work students dress appropriately as professionals when they go on field placement. In terms of gender, an example of the institutional aspect might be the system of educational policies and practices which restrict womens' access to tertiary education, and therefore function to confine them to housewife roles or lower status occupations.

Application of ideological analysis to radical casework practice

Using the concept of ideology and analysis of these three aspects (practical, theoretical and institutional) provides a convenient breakdown for the radical caseworker to locate the specific influence of social, economic, and cultural structures on the lives of individual people.

1   First, the significance of the *practices of individuals* in reinforcing the dominant social structures is highlighted. So when analysing the client's problem situation it is useful for the caseworker to be aware of particular customs, routines or roles performed that may reflect internalised social expectations rather than personal choice or that may simply reflect an institutionalised lack of choices in that situation. For example, when clients seek the

assistance of a social worker this may be because this is the socially expected or normal pathway to receive help for their particular situation, the internalised social expectation, rather than their purely personal inclination. Or they may approach a voluntary welfare agency primarily because they believe that this is the last resort for people in their impoverished situation; that is, there are no other choices available. In gender terms, another example is the mother who assumes prime responsibility for domestic duties because she believes this is what all women do and should do. Nor is she able to enlist her husband's help around the home because he refuses to assist. This not only helps to reinforce her personal social position as housewife, but also the social institution of the traditional family.

2   Secondly, ideological analysis can be used to focus on the *socially originated myths or beliefs* the person holds. If the social structure does manifest itself in personal beliefs, then these ideas themselves may be a partial cause of the person's problem. In other words, it is not necessarily victims per se who are blamable, but it may be the social myths they believe which are self-defeating for them. Therefore it may be useful for radical caseworkers to discuss with clients their thinking in relation to any mythical beliefs, or stereotyped or prejudiced views, since these may indicate areas in which they are more socially than personally influenced. For example, people who believe their only recourse is to regularly seek material aid may be so doing because they have learnt this idea from their social group. (This social influence lies behind the 'culture of poverty' idea that sees a culture of customs and beliefs associated with being poor. This culture, of course, functions to keep them poor.) Another example, related to gender, is the belief that women who don't want children are not normal females, or that childless women are not fully adult or mature females (Wearing, 1984:42–4). This belief ensures that women will keep having children, often meaning that they will be restricted to mothering roles (because of a structural lack of other social opportunities for mothers), and thus reinforcing existing gender roles and institutions.

There is a further point regarding social myths which needs to be addressed. Whether or not a belief is true or false has nothing to do with whether it functions as a social myth or not, but its truth or falsity may say something further about social conditions. A mythical belief may in fact be generally *true* because it is existing ideological practices, beliefs and structures which have brought about the particular situation. Let me illustrate. Take the belief or myth that non-white people are less intelligent than white people. This idea may function as a 'false' myth, but also may be partly 'true'. If intelligence has been measured by tests derived in white Western cultures (and this is how intelligence is defined), or the non-white people tested are less educated than the whites who are tested, then there is every chance that they will perform less well and be deemed less intelligent. However, this is a *false* idea given that the concept of intelligence and its measurement are problematic and there exists no consensual agreement that whites are more intelligent than non-whites. As well, given different conditions—culturally relevant tests or equivalent educational experiences—the results may be quite different. The central point is that in general a myth is a myth because, although people consider that it is its truth (or falsity) in which they believe, the real function of the social belief is masked. The real function of the belief in white intellectual superiority is that it justifies social practices which deny non-whites jobs or education, and thus helps keep white populations more powerful. The myth also needs to be maintained if this state of affairs is to continue.

This is an important point for radical caseworkers because it means there is a need, when working with individual people, to differentiate between myths which have little basis in reality and those which are true because accompanying social conditions have brought them about. The strategies needed to deal with each may be different. The former may simply require a questioning and challenging of ideas. The latter may necessitate that as well as some changes in the person's situation so the effects of the ideology can be demonstrably reversed on a material level.

3 There is a third way in which ideological analysis may be useful to the radical caseworker. This is by pointing up how the *practices and beliefs of other significant people* in the person's life may be important. They may influence the person directly, through daily interaction, or indirectly, by helping to preserve structures which socially embody such thinking and behaviour. Take, for example, the housewife who does not subscribe to the dominant view, and believes that she is and should be capable of undertaking tertiary education. Any contrary beliefs of women at her tennis club may influence her by undermining her confidence. Their refusal to help with child minding so she can attend classes, as well as negative gossip about her and the state of her marriage (which may also be implied by their husbands to hers) may be aimed at ensuring that she does not become too different from them.

4 The last way in which ideological analysis can be useful is by looking at *social institutions* themselves and their direct effects (the system of roles and practices, expectations and cultural

beliefs which sustains a certain pattern of arrangements) on the life of the individual. The concept of ideology shows that there is a clear link between broader social arrangements and the thoughts, actions and life choices of individual people. For example, from knowledge of particular social policies, the caseworker can trace specific effects on a client. This is most obviously the case when working in the statutory income security area, and seeing how policy changes regarding entitlements affect the income and welfare of individual people. Some institutions may imply certain value perspectives and thus implicitly reward some behaviour and devalue others. For example, some housewives may place undue importance on playing the 'hostess' role because they believe domestic duties are the only acceptable role open to them within the traditional institution of the nuclear family, and therefore the only way they can achieve status and social recognition is to excel at such a role.

SOCIAL CONTROL

The radical interest in social control stems from the criticism that social work upholds existing social conditions which actually disadvantage clients. The process of social control refers to the ways in which a society ensures that its members behave in socially approved and accepted ways (Robertson, 1977:58-9). If these norms are contravened there are sanctions which apply (Cowger & Atherton, 1977).

The professional caseworker is seen as contributing to social control by subtly holding clients in powerless positions and reinforcing the identities ascribed to them by the dominant order. The *professional ideology* inherent in social work training, socialisation and culture is a major means of achieving this control. The broad principle for radical caseworkers to follow in tracing the effects of professional ideology in controlling themselves and clients is to analyse how any professional practices or beliefs regarded as normal or desirable or expected may function to maintain the profession's status and/or its dominance over clients.

The disabling function of professional ideology is well noted by Illich (1977). The theoretical aspect of this ideology is the belief that professionals are experts who know more than clients about their problem situation and the means to deal with it. In practice this means that they assume a professional expert role, often distancing themselves from clients, and in the process distancing clients from the means to rectify their situations. The institutional aspect of this professional ideology is the arrangement whereby professionals act in an entrepreneurial 'middle person' role, effectively controlling the means and resources for problem alleviation. In some instances they may even function to disable clients as self-help becomes less possible, and potential clients must conform to the expectations of the professional (that clients are unable to help themselves) in order to receive help from the professional.

There are other specific professional ideologies embodied in many of the traditional ethics of casework. We discussed that of 'individualisation' in chapter 2. Although I argued there that it is important that the radical caseworker respect the individual person, as is embodied in this ethic, there still remains a danger that constant attention to individual problems can lead to an assumption that all problems are primarily individually-based. Thus radical caseworkers need to be vigilant that they do not mistake the *ethic* of individualisation for the *ideology* of individualisation.

Other ethics such as 'objectivity' and 'self-determination' may mask professional ideologies which subtly control clients. The rationale for professional objectivity may be the belief that clients are best helped by someone they see as a respected authority who is not emotionally involved with them. Like many functional myths, this has true and false components, but it is the actual social effect of this idea that is important. On an institutional level, professionals who act in this way may find it easier to get jobs because it is felt they can command respect. Clients may act in complementary ways when confronted with a professional playing an objective role. They may defer to the professional, uncritically believe what they are told, and find that they receive more positive attention when they behave in this way.

The ideology of 'self-determination' can function in a similar way. The belief that clients should be able to make their own decisions without undue direction from the caseworker is a laudable idea. Unfortunately there are false elements. The belief that people can make their own decisions ignores the fact that all individuals are constrained within a social environment by a huge array of factors such as interpersonal, legal and bureaucratic constraints. Not only that, a belief in self-determination ignores the fact that it is often the professional person, not the client, who has the power to determine some of the rules. It is also the professional who commands the interpersonal respect of the client, due to the way the professional role is socially constructed. The ideology of self-determination also masks the fact that many social work clients are involuntary.

Professional ideologies may also manifest and maintain sexist ideologies. Hearn (1985) shows how ideologies among the semi-professions and their striving to professional status reflect ideologies about femininity and acceptable 'hand-maiden to men' roles. Professional social work ideologies about consensus and the denial of aggression also contribute to the 'feminine' status of social work, in particular, casework. I am not arguing here that feminine characteristics are not desirable characteristics (indeed many feminists reaffirm the value of traditionally female characteristics such as nurturance and caring). What is masked by these ideologies, however, is that some professions may simply be a form of institutionalised patriarchy, and in this sense will impose sanctions on those (both clients and members of the profession) who do not fit this mould. This is particularly the case with individuals who do not fit the expected traditional family norm. For several decades single parent (usually mother) families were considered inherently problematic, as were children raised in families where the mother worked (that is, 'latch-key' children). Ideologies of deviance are also operating here. However, control is also assisted by group ideologies.

Control by other groups

The analysis of professional ideologies and the processes by which the social work profession controls members and clients in complementary conformity can be applied to power relations between other groups which affect the lives of individual people. One way for the radical caseworker to apply this principle of social control through ideologies is to analyse any situation which involves power imbalances between different social groups in this way. For example, the dominance and, in some cases, exploitation of monied over working classes, men over women, full professions over semi-professions, adult over child, able-bodied person over person with disability, white races over black, Western cultures over non-Western can be explained through an analysis of *specific group ideologies*—the beliefs, behaviours and organised systems which maintain these inequities of power.

Sanctions can, of course, be applied between groups who have ostensibly equal power, such as between two groups who are generally both regarded as disadvantaged, but who rely on the distinctions between them to maintain their status or social identity. An example would be two ethnic minority groups who are both disadvantaged because of their migrant status, but who steadfastly refuse to co-operate as this would involve the dissolution of barriers which are considered important to the group's survival. It has been noted only too regularly that not all disadvantaged groups necessarily identify with each other nor are they prepared to collectively seek social change (for example, see Pemberton, 1982:33). One fictitious

incident which illustrates this issue particularly poignantly was
quoted in the movie about FBI confrontation of the Ku Klux Klan,
Mississippi Burning. In it, Gene Hackman reminisces about his
father, a small-time Southern farmer who murdered the donkey of
a neighbouring black farmer. Owning a donkey was considered a
sign of success, but it was not pure personal jealousy which motivated this white farmer. As he remarks to his son, 'Who are you
better than if you're not better than the blacks?' Hackman ponders,
'Maybe my daddy just didn't know poverty was killing him.'
    One of the very powerful effects of social control is that it is the
most disadvantaged groups who turn on each other, rather than
locating the blame fairly and squarely on the shoulders of a broad
social system. It is important, therefore, for the radical caseworker to
see that prejudices or mythical beliefs that individual members of
disadvantaged classes might hold are not necessarily reflections on
the group. Rather, they may be a reflection of dominant ideologies
which use these differences to maintain their own group's survival.

Control within the social group

The social control analysis also points up how members of a social
group exercise control over each other in order to maintain the
accepted identity and relative social status of that group. Control
does not only come from within through internalised norms, or from
outside through broad social restrictions. Members of one's own
peer group with whom one identifies can be powerful controllers.
This is an important point because it may be from the client's own peer
group that the greatest obstacles to addressing the problem emerge. For
example, members of a client group may negatively sanction those
who demand their rights for fear that professionals will refuse them
all further help, or they may accuse outspoken clients of 'abusing
the system' or 'jumping the queue'. Class divisions may be maintained
by working class beliefs that middle class people are more 'brainy'
and thus have rights to education and higher paid jobs. Similarly
they may hold ideologies which stigmatise education as 'just useless
theory' and those who aspire to it as not really any good because they
don't know anything about the 'real' world. Those who seek continued
education at tertiary level and beyond may be castigated as 'professional students' who are not contributing to their community.

ANTI-OPPRESSION

Early radical critiques stressed the ideal of 'protecting the individual
from the system'. This idea became more generalised to encompass

a stance against oppression, or situations in which any group or person is disadvantaged in order to serve the interests of the more advantaged. The concept of ideology is of further use here in pointing up the specific ways in which personal or group beliefs and practices may contribute to the oppression of that person or group. There are, however, other theories which can add to our understanding of social oppression, namely, labelling theory, and some aspects of feminist analysis.

Feminism and personal liberation

The relevance of feminist theory to social work is now well documented (Brook & Davis, 1985; Dominelli & McLeod, 1989), particularly because of the congruence of socialist and feminist analysis regarding the formation of individual consciousness by social and cultural institutions (Marchant, 1986; Wearing, 1986). However, where the feminist view differs is in showing that it does not logically follow that women's identities must be socially dictated (Berlin & Kravetz, 1981:4). Thus feminist analysis is personally and socially liberating (Bricker-Jenkins & Hooyman, 1986) in that it assumes womens' ultimate ability to free themselves from gender-related restrictions. This of course is one of the major aims of the feminist movement. This non-determinist aspect of feminist analysis is of great value to the radical caseworker. Although moulded by social expectation and structural arrangements, the individual may be able to overcome some restrictions and exercise personal choice. For example, awareness of the exact ways in which clients are oppressed may give pointers to the exact ways in which they may be liberated. This is fundamentally what the process of conscientisation or consciousness-raising is about. This will be addressed in far greater detail in the chapter where we discuss strategies and techniques. At this stage, however, it is important to note that the radical stance against oppression should be enacted by enabling personal liberation.

Social labelling

The notion that deviant groups often become and remain that way through a process of social labelling is useful when combined with the concept of ideology. It highlights specific aspects of social attitudes to, and beliefs about, deviant groups. The theory can also be applied to any relatively powerless or minority group or individual like legal offenders, welfare recipients, sexual deviants or people with disabilities. Frequently, powerful groups hold attitudes towards minority groups which are socially distancing in some ways. Typically they might look upon them with pity, guilt or shame, or act towards them with over-compensating behaviours (Goffman, 1963). The function of this process is to socially distance the holder of the attitude from the object of it. The holder of the attitude is made to feel more normal, or acceptable, in proportion to the degree that the object of the stigma is made to feel more different and unacceptable. The object of the attitude is thus forced into acting in accordance with the labelling, since the behaviour will be interpreted by others to fit with this role. In this way, social expectations and interactions may, in fact, amplify deviant behaviour. For example, people with disabilities may become more disabled because they are seen by others as individuals who always need help, are treated accordingly, and are therefore not given opportunities or the appropriate resources to become independent. They begin to see themselves as dependent and therefore become that way because they do not try, nor learn to be anything different. As well, any attempt at independent behaviour may be interpreted as an inability to graciously accept their limitations.

It may therefore be useful for radical caseworkers to be aware of situations where the process of labelling may be occurring either through personally held beliefs, or through particular practices which prolong and support stigmatising attitudes. A person's negative self-perceptions may be a pointer. The worker's own distancing attitudes may be another. Policies which draw attention to, and restrict, rather than create opportunities for minority groups may be yet another instance of labelling.

SOCIAL CRITIQUE

The radical analysis of the social control functions of social work, and the awareness of the oppression of less powerful groups results in the necessity to question and criticise social arrangements which contribute to these processes. Since apparently benign institutions like social welfare may covertly oppress or disadvantage those they are supposedly helping, other social institutions may also have similar hidden functions. There are a number of ways in which the radical caseworker can apply this critical assumption.

Beneficiaries

First, it may be useful to note who benefits from a particular situation. Exactly whose (which person's/people's, group's or institution's) interests are actually being served by the situation at hand? This may be hidden, or may be quite open. For example, it is openly acknowledged that schooling performs important socialising functions for society, as well as being for educational purposes. It is less openly acknowledged that keeping young people at school for maximum periods (although possibly educating them better) functions to keep them out of the ranks of the unemployed longer, and therefore they are less of a social problem. For a caseworker dealing with an individual problem situation, it may be that a parent who seeks advice about whether her or his child should remain at school or not is not really concerned about the educational welfare of the child, but more about the potential parental problems if the child becomes unemployed. These, of course, are real and legitimate concerns, but they should be directly addressed by the caseworker as the parent's social concerns, rather than the child's educational ones.

Social function

A second similar way of questioning social arrangements is to immediately look for the social function that a particular situation performs. As with the above example, although schooling obviously functions educationally, there are social aspects which are part of the educational function and also extra to it. As many studies show (for example, Stanley & Wise, 1983) succeeding at school usually involves some academic achievement as well as some degree of conformity to gender stereotypes inherent in the schooling system. Sometimes people may mistake the social conformity as being necessary for the academic achievement or, in extreme cases, that they are the same thing. As with the foregoing example, for the caseworker dealing with an individual problem situation, it may be that a parent who seeks casework advice, about whether the child should leave school early or continue on, may really be more concerned about the child's continued attendance at school for the social (rather than educational) functions this performs. Again, this is a legitimate enough worry. However, the parent's concern needs to be dealt with at this level—how the child and parent will deal with the social implications of leaving school (for example, possible unemployment)—rather than ignoring this worry and looking only at the educational issues.

Conflicting interest

Thirdly, a socially critical approach may be enhanced by looking for the involvement of any different or conflicting interest groups in a given situation. There may be more than one party or group which benefits from a situation, and sometimes their interests may converge, and sometimes they may conflict. They may therefore resist changes instigated by the caseworker as their interests are jeopardised. Referring to our example, there are a number of parties with interests in the institution of schooling—teachers, children, the government, employers, parents, to name some. The situation of children leaving school early may benefit some employers because they gain young cheap labour. It may benefit some parents for the same reason in that they can have an immediate input into their own financial support. It may benefit some sectors of the government which are concerned about government over-spending on the education system. It may not benefit other sectors of the government which are concerned about inflated unemployment figures. It may not benefit teachers, who will presumably have fewer jobs if there are fewer students. It may not benefit some parents, who would prefer to keep their children financially dependent upon them. The radical caseworkers' analysis needs to take into account whose interests will be jeopardised by their intervention and how this may be addressed in order to deal effectively on a social level with the person's problem situation. Continuing the school example, and using our knowledge of traditional sex-role expectations, it may be that the parents' interests conflict with the student's, regarding the issue of the child's staying at school. The mother may wish the child to remain at school and financially dependent to keep her or him at home longer and therefore maintain her own role as mother. The father may wish the child to leave school to work, and so ease the financial burden on him. There may be additional conflicting pressure brought to bear on the child because teachers are encouraging him or her to remain at school. In addition, there may be some government policies which encourage young people to stay at school (such as lower unemployment benefit rates for people under sixteen).

Behaviour

Fourthly, an awareness of the ways in which interested parties actively preserve or cause the situation may be useful in indicating aspects of the person's situation which need to be changed. Again using our above example of schooling, a particular employer may run recruitment drives among local school kids to ensure cheap labour. The father may encourage the child to go and see this employer. The child's mother may appeal to the school teachers to take some action against this employer. This one example of socially critical analysis indicates several points of specific action for the radical caseworker.

SOCIAL AND PERSONAL CHANGE

The radical social work commitment to analysing the social structure
and working against the oppressive elements identified by this
analysis, leads logically to a belief in the ideal of social change.
There are two aspects to this belief: that social change is necessary
or desirable; and that social change is possible. The change aimed
for is a less exploitative, more egalitarian, non-patriarchal society.
The aim is both to breakdown such specific structures, but also to
establish alternative structures in their place. For radical social
workers this may take the form of breaking down patriarchal and
professional dominance. For radical caseworkers working at the
individual level, it may involve counteracting the personal effects
of oppression, reducing self-blame, and re-establishing self-esteem
and personal autonomy and power. In this endeavour, '. . . a framework of cultural diversity is more illuminating than an uncritical
acceptance of the ideology of "normal" ' (Bailey & Brake,
1975:10).

In other words, in meeting the ideal of social change, a social
analysis which is aware of, and allows for social and cultural
diversity is mandatory. This is an important point, because much of
the early radical literature ignored the issue of cultural differences,
and concentrated mainly on class (and later, gender) differences. A
truly radical approach, however, should also take into account
cultural exploitation, and the maintenance of the dominance of some
cultural systems over others. There should therefore be a cross-cul-
tural and anti-racist aspect to radical casework (see Petruchenia,
1990).

Unfortunately it would be unrealistic to argue that there are not
some limitations on the social change aspirations of radical social
workers, particularly on the day-to-day level of working with individual people. Social workers, like other workers, are employed by,
and to an extent trapped within an institutional structure of welfare
(Bailey & Brake, 1980:8–9). It has also been suggested that structural changes may be limited by the desires and abilities of welfare
recipients themselves. For instance, Pemberton (1982) argues that
welfare consumers in Australia have not always been successful at
political action, and often do not want to 'collectivise' with other
socially deviant groups, such as criminals. Sometimes, as is the case
with some groups of unemployed people in Australia, the request
has been for reformist, not revolutionary changes. In extending this
point, it has been argued that the radical work that *is* possible may
only be relevant to a small proportion of the typical social worker's
caseload (Clarke, 1976:504–5). Therefore, whatever change is

achieved by radical social workers is likely to be small (Pemberton, 1982:32–3).

On the other hand, Galper (1980:109) argues that it is reasonable to expect a low level of structural change, given the modest amount of radical activity in society generally. However, as radical practice advances, new possibilities may emerge. The existence of the present limitations may simply mean that it is also part of the radical task to examine more closely the reasons for the constraints. It is likely that they are partly due to an ideology of oppression, causing workers and welfare consumers both to believe in their own impotence because they are actually alienated from the sources of power. This ideology requires closer investigation and possible challenging. As Galper (1980:118) says, a radical perspective:

> . . . involves helping people to re-examine the widely shared assumption that we are unable to create change. People would be more ready to examine a radical analysis if they were not blocked by the sense that such an analysis will not serve them as a basis for action. The anticipation of having no way to act on the basis of a radical analysis limits the possibility of becoming more radical.

In the preceding sections we have seen some indication of how social and cultural institutions, through a process of ideology, can be oppressive to powerless groups and individuals. Change may happen as they seek liberation from, for example, their own beliefs or practices which support these oppressive structures. Thus personal change is an adjunct of social change. As Wilson (1980:39) points out, this also applies the other way around. Social change cannot be brought about unless individual people feel that the changed politics will answer their personal needs. Obviously the personal and social changes desired must be congruent.

Alienation

The concept of alienation is useful in elaborating the importance of the idea of change in a radical stance. As defined by Keefe (1984:146) alienation is 'the condition in capitalist industrial society in which the self and significant aspects of the physical and social environment are experienced as estranged and out of control'. In this way personal alienation is a condition which results from the way capitalism is experienced so in order to

> . . . cope with capitalist society, people begin to equate the human condition with the state of alienation. They believe it is natural to feel like cogs in a wheel, to exploit rather than to love others, and to despise themselves. (Longres, 1981:87)

In this way the experience of alienation also helps maintain the existing capitalist structure. Alienated people perceive their world as out of control, unchangeable, and therefore feel powerless to act upon it. Thus radical caseworkers may need to identify the influence of alienation in their clients' lives by recognising the ideological functions of beliefs about powerlessness, or the immutability of the status quo (Galper, 1980:40–1).

Historical analysis

Let us move on to a further point regarding social change. Another implication of the idea of social change for the radical caseworker when analysing the individual person's situation is the need for historical analysis. Both socialist and feminist analyses are based on extensive examination of past conditions and their role in determining present capitalist and patriarchal structures. Mills (1959:179) emphasises the necessity of historical analysis in conjunction with structural analysis in understanding the individual person:

> Adequate understanding requires that we grasp the interplay of these intimate settings with their larger structural framework, and that we take into account the transformations of this framework, and the consequent effects upon milieux. When we understand social structures and structural changes as they bear upon more intimate scenes and experiences, we are able to understand the causes of individual conduct and feelings of . . . men [sic] in specific milieux . . .

For this reason, an analysis of structure must incorporate an analysis of structural *changes*; that is, how social structures have changed over time.

Such an analysis underscores two principles useful to the radical caseworker's understanding of the social situation of individual clients. First, historical analysis shows that present social conditions are not necessarily immutable, but that change is possible. If existing social conditions are understood as having developed as a response to past conditions then, if these conditions no longer exist, the corresponding structures may also be changeable. In this way it may be helpful for radical caseworkers to be aware of past social conditions which might have determined the person's present way of life. They may then need to establish whether this mode of living is still necessary or appropriate, and what present conditions may motivate change.

Secondly, historical analysis of social developments often reveals a record of different beliefs, practices and institutions which appear inexplicable in the light of present-day experience. However, when viewed in historical context they may seem quite appropriate. This

principle of what I shall term 'historical relativity' highlights the
fact that individual people must be understood in historical context.
A person's problem can only be fully explained by a knowledge of
the general social conditions that may have been an influence in
past significant periods (Carr, 1961:55). In this way, behaviour that
is today viewed as unnecessary, may emanate from attitudes that
made it appropriate in past social conditions, and therefore is
wrongly assessed if seen against a backdrop of current fashions,
Callan (1985:122), for example, notes the experience of cohabiting
couples who married over a decade ago. Those who decided to
marry primarily because of parental pressure might today be viewed
as overly compliant. However, past social attitudes towards cohab-
itation were more strongly negative than today. Social institutions,
in particular through banks and lending practices, supported negative
attitudes more directly. Under these conditions, when pressures to
marry *were* significant, it is understandable that couples would have
perceived these pressures as important enough to motivate them to
marry. It may have been much more difficult *not* to conform to
marriage expectations in the past than now. Therefore these couples
should not be regarded as over-conforming, to the same degree that
couples who marry because of parental pressure today may be
thought overly compliant.

Mills (1959:180) extends this point to argue that even specific
assessments of the influence of a person's emotional background
must be seen in relation to the social conditions of that time:

> The relevance of earlier experience, the 'weight' of childhood in the
> psychology of adult character is itself relative to the type of
> childhood and the type of social biography that prevail in various
> societies.

As an example Mills shows how the role of father in forming
personality must also be seen in the context of specific types of
families, and in terms of the particular place that family occupies
in the particular social structure of that time (1959:180) This example can be used to illustrate how the principle of historical relativity
might be applied by the radical caseworker. In seeking to understand
a male client whose childhood was dominated by his father, the man
and social worker may need to discuss what the role of father
entailed in the man's particular childhood class and culture. If it
was normal that fathers dominated, there may have been other social
and economic practices, as well as family roles, that supported this
domination. As well, family expectations may have been a dominant
socialising force in that particular social structure. In the context of
these social conditions, the client's experience may be more expli-
cable. Thus, for example, his present inability to make decisions

independently from his father, may be understandable. Applying the principle of historical relativity in this type of case may mean that the man's present behaviour is not deemed to demonstrate personal inadequacy, simply because it is not considered desirable in present social terms.

It may be more accurate to judge this behaviour as historically acceptable, but at present undesirable, and deal with it on the basis of this analysis.

5   Assessment

Now that we have outlined and discussed some specific working concepts of how the social structure directly affects the lives of individual people, what do these concepts tell us about the causes of the problem situations in which people find themselves? How do we actually determine and evaluate what are the causes of our clients' problems? It is the aim of this chapter to discuss the particular issues that are involved in making these sorts of judgements, and to develop some guidelines which will assist the radical caseworker in making these assessments.

The assessment of problems is of singular importance in radical casework, because, as Goldberg (1974:150) says 'Definition of a problem is a potent force in determining action to alleviate it, for the way in which a problem is formulated places constraints on the range of alternatives from which a solution can be drawn'. The way we define and interpret problems then will define the way we deal with them. If we are particularly interested in finding radical ways to practice casework, then we must make doubly certain that we find radical ways to assess problems.

First though, let us clarify what is traditionally meant by assessment in casework. This is generally agreed to involve the formation of professional judgements, evaluations, opinions or interpretations about the particular causes and types of problems experienced by clients. Assessment is an important part of the casework process because it helps specify how aspects of the person's situation function in each case to give rise to the particular problem at hand

(Northern, 1982:60–1). It is essentially the phase of casework helping where a theory is formed about the particular causes of a
particular person's particular situation. In this sense it is the point
at which we move on from our understanding of broad theory and
knowledge and begin to apply this to explain a specific situation.
This, of course, is the precise point at which things become tricky,
as it is always problematic to apply the general to the specific and
emerge with an explanation which can account for all details. It is,
on the other hand, regarded as one of the essential tools of trade
for a professional person and it is, therefore, essential that we pay
special attention to this aspect of the radical caseworker's work.
However, the stage of assessment is still theoretical in the sense that
it is about understanding a person's problem situation rather than
intervening in it.

There are at least two components of the assessment process
which most casework literature refers to. First, it is often necessary
to determine which types of problems are appropriate for a social
casework approach, as opposed to those which may be more effectively handled by other methods such as medical care or community
action. Secondly, in order to simplify the task of defining appropriate action to be taken, categories of problem types are sometimes
devised so that intervention can be matched accordingly later
(Loewenberg, 1983). In this chapter we will deal with assessment
in radical casework by first looking at how we determine what types
of casework problems might be most suitable to a radical approach;
that is, what types of problems might be primarily structurally
caused. Then, based on the concepts discussed in the preceding chapter,
we devise a typology of structural causes of personal problems.

DIFFERENTIATING PERSONAL AND STRUCTURAL

As I have said earlier, a major difference between traditional and
radical conceptions of problems is the degree to which the social
structure is believed to be a cause of personal problems. More
traditional approaches tend to see problems as individually based,
with the social environment relegated to the background as a complicating factor. A radical perspective views personal problems as
primarily structurally based, although complicated by purely personal factors.

Two points which need to be addressed here are whether a radical
approach assumes that *all* problems are structurally caused and
exactly how individual and structural factors, which normally interact in any given situation, can be clearly differentiated and assessed.
The best answer to the first point is that not *all* personal problems

are *totally* structurally caused. But while personal factors also contribute to personal problems, there is always a structural element in any experienced problem. The structural element will always interplay with personal factors such as biography, current life events, emotional and psychological characteristics, genetic inheritance, physical health, and so on to create a unique personal situation. For the radical caseworker this must always be noted and not downplayed in any assessment of the situation. (See the assessment guide checklist in the Appendix for a complete list of personal, social and structural factors which may need to be noted.)

Having assumed that there is an interplay of personal and structural elements, the crucial issue then for the radical caseworker is to differentiate between personal and structural factors, and how they exacerbate aspects of the problem. To do this it helps to classify personal problems into two main groups: those in which personal factors predominate, and those in which structural factors predominate.

It is unlikely that problems will fall neatly into one or the other category. In fact it makes much better sense to use the idea of a continuum to help differentiate some of the complexities involved (McIntyre, 1982). For our analysis, located at one end of the continuum are situations in which individual factors dominate. At the other end are those in which structural factors are more important. The relative position on the continuum may help indicate the proportionate type of intervention appropriate in each instance.

The concept of a continuum of problem types where structural factors have varying significance also helps highlight the idea that even though personal problems may be structurally caused, the way the structural causes interplay with individual factors can create uniquely experienced problems, which need to be handled as just that. To illustrate the two ends of the continuum, McIntyre (1982:201–2) provides an example of two young people presenting with low self-esteem from unemployment. It may be clear in one case that the depression is secondary to the structural situation of poor employment opportunities for youth. In the other case it may emerge that the situation is complicated by the girl's guilt about working, in view of the dependence of a disabled mother. Although discussion of social pressures on her may help resolve her feelings of depression about lack of work, her guilt regarding her mother's care may still remain, and casework efforts to provide alternative care for her mother rejected. For this aspect of the case it may be more appropriate to concentrate on some of the more personal aspects of the situation, such as the girl's relationship with her mother, the personal stress she is experiencing, and her concerns about alternative care.

Let us examine some specific examples. In the first instance, feminist theory may prove useful. Adrienne Rich, in discussing the meaning of mothering, distinguishes between the experience (the subjective experience of mothering independent of that caused by male domination) and the institution (aspects of the experience which developed under patriarchy) (Eisenstein, 1984:70). This differentiation between the experience and institution also helps to separate the aspects of a situation that are a result of personal uniqueness on the one hand and social acceptability on the other. In this way, for example, a woman's perceived problem of unsatisfactory mothering can be initially assessed by noting to what extent the problem is caused by factors exclusive to the woman (such as having been abused as a child) or by common social expectations of mothers (such as feeling the need to be infinitely nurturant).

A second example, using the phenomenon of death denial, also helps illustrate the distinction. From research with terminally ill cancer patients, Kellehear and Fook (1989) noted that patients' ostensible denial—unwillingness to discuss or even acknowledge their imminent death—was motivated by a number of reasons. Some of these were more personal in nature, in that the denial of death helped defend people against unwanted anxiety or emotional conflict. Other reasons were more sociological—the denial was more an attempt to avoid the negative social role associated with dying, rather than the idea of death itself. In these cases the death was acknowledged to selected significant people but not to others, therefore it appeared like denial in some instances. For example, in one case, a man openly discussed his imminent death with family members, but denied it to his physician. In the patient's reasoning, he was attempting to socially reinforce the doctor's treatment efforts by not letting him think he had given up hope of a cure. In another case the impending death was freely discussed with a hospital researcher, but not admitted to family members, for fear of upsetting family relationships. Both these cases of apparent psychodynamic denial are more accurately seen as examples of sociological 'role distancing'; that is, avoiding negative social roles. This is a type of sociological, rather than psychological denial.

As well, there may be other, more structural reasons for denying death. These relate to a fear of negative social images of dying, that often might date back to past history and cultures. For example, isolation and contamination may be feared as a result of medical images of incurable disease and aged disability. There may be a fear of violence or deprivation brought about by war images of destruction and suffering (Kellehear, 1984). In these cases the denial is better viewed as an avoidance of negative social images, rather than as a psychological defence.

The distinction between the social avoidance of the dying role and the psychodynamic denial of death directly correspond to Rich's distinction between institution and experience. Using it can indicate different strategies for intervention depending on which aspect is predominant. In the case of death denial, if the denial is primarily performing psychodynamic functions, therapeutic or counselling techniques, which aim at reducing emotional conflict or stress, may need to be employed. If the avoidance is primarily social, strategies which address these factors, such as making social preparation for dying, and dealing with people's socially derived perceptions of their role, may be more important. (Specific socially oriented strategies for death denial are discussed in detail by Kellehear and Fook (1989).

Now that we are clear about some preliminary ways to begin assessing the interplay of personal and structural factors, let us look more closely at the ways structural factors can cause personal problems.

STRUCTURAL CAUSES OF PERSONAL PROBLEMS

As we have established, there are a number of distinct ways in which the socio-economic structure influences personally experienced problems: through ideological restrictions; through processes of social control; through social labelling processes; and as a result of social change. Before we take them one by one, it is also important to define what we mean by 'cause' of a problem. There is a variety of levels of causality, some more direct than others, Causation may or may not be one way; that is, structural problems do not necessarily always predate personal problems.

First, structural factors may indirectly complicate or exacerbate existing personal problems. For example, the problem of physical disability (say the loss of both legs) resulting from a car accident may be worsened because of the lack of facilities for people with disabilities, and the negative labelling attitudes of other people. This may in turn cause a person with disabilities to lose both social independence and personal confidence. So what was essentially a personally experienced problem (physical disability) in the first instance may become a more severe personally experienced problem because of social deficiencies in the way the disability is addressed.

Secondly, structural factors may actually cause personal problems more directly, in that the personal problem is really a symptom manifestation of, or reaction to, structural conditions (as the anti-psychiatrists were fond of saying, insanity is simply a sane reaction to an insane world (Agel, 1971)). A person's unemployment may simply be a symptom of current economic downturn. Or to use the earlier example, a person's lack of adjustment to loss of both legs may be a direct result of the lack of appropriate social resources to deal with it.

Thirdly, structural factors may cause personal problems in a deeper way, by influencing the perceptions and choices that individual people have in their lives; that is, by *socialising* them. Dying people who simply wish to avoid the unpleasant aspects of the dying role may have no choice but to appear as if that they are neurotically denying their own death, because there is no socially acknowledged and acceptable way to die. A housewife who is desperately dissatisfied with her life may feel trapped because she cannot imagine any other lifestyle. It may be more difficult to adjust to the loss of your legs through accident because there are few role models of successful people with disabilities, and you may believe it is impossible to achieve your previously held goals.

Fourthly, definitions of normality and deviance are structurally and politically determined. Personal problems may therefore simply exist because they are socially defined as problems, not necessarily because of any inherent deficiency. Much work has been done on the problem of mental illness which shows how definitions of illness vary between culture, historical period, and gender (Agel, 1971). The problem of mental illness then may simply exist because it suits the interests of certain social groups for it to be seen that way. Again, a physical disability is not necessarily a personal problem, but is defined as one since most of our categories of normality assume an intact physical body.

Lastly, structural factors can most directly cause personal problems by determining the material conditions under which individual people live. Many supporting mothers are in poverty as a direct result of disadvantaging family laws. People with physical disabilities may be unable to assume a fulfilling lifestyle because of a lack of relevant social resources.

In any assessment of an individual's problems, all these direct and indirect levels of causation may operate.

Ideological restrictions

The category of problems resulting from ideological restrictions includes problems which result from aspects of prevailing ideologies we have already discussed. They include restrictions on behaviour, belief, and institutional arrangements.

Restrictive behaviour

These include problems resulting from stereotyped roles, role conflicts and role socialisation.

Stereotyped roles are obviously problematic in that they can limit
personal growth and capabilities. Feminist literature provides copi-
ous examples of how sex-role stereotypes cause personal hardship.
However, any stereotyped role which a person assumes (or is
assumed to take) because of social expectation can also be problematic. Most notable are age, racial, class and occupational stereotypes.

Conflicts between social roles or between individual people performing conflicting social roles may cause personally experienced
problems. For example, some women may be unable to successfully
resolve the conflicting expectations between career and motherhood.
Role conflict may be a source of guilt for people seeking the best
care for ageing parents. They may be unable to care for them in
their own homes because of obligations to their own children, and
cannot therefore fulfil both roles of dutiful children and dutiful
parents at the same time. Within the nuclear family there may be
direct conflict between the father (breadwinner role) and mother
(nurturing role) over issues involving discipline and finance of the
children.

Role socialisation or behaviour that results from learning certain
social roles, can also cause problems. Roles that involve a 'learned
helplessness' (Sturvidant, 1980:123) are a good example of this.
Such roles might include female, patient or old-aged roles, where a
socially acceptable aspect of the role is powerlessness and dependency. The problem is that dependent, powerless behaviour, although
clearly expected, condoned and reinforced in certain social roles, is
often problematic in other life situations. Other problems that can
come out of this are depression and negative self-views which can
also be seen as mental health problems, and which frequently relate
to aspects of women's role socialisation such as the role expected
of a married woman (Gottlieb, 1980).

Restrictive beliefs

Problems can occur with restrictive beliefs in three ways: through
unchangeable false beliefs, belief conflicts, and socialised beliefs.

Rigidly holding mythical beliefs that consequently restrict role
options or perpetuate self-destructive ideas may be the cause of
many personal problems. Examples of such beliefs are that people
with disabilities cannot live independently; that education is wasted
on women; or that 'nice' women are not assertive.

Problems caused by conflicts between beliefs are those which may directly involve more than one person, or become internalised. A person might hold conflicting beliefs because of changing belief systems, conflicting roles, or simultaneous membership in different groups with incompatible value systems. Conceivably these sorts of conflicts could occur in situations such as when mature-age people seek re-education or career change; cultural conflicts experienced through migration; or 'generation-gap' conflicts between adolescent and parental values.

Lastly, the beliefs engendered through particular role social-isations may require the learning of personal characteristics which are actually self-defeating for the person both in and outside that role. As cited earlier, self-defeating attitudes, poor self-esteem or self-blame can result from the chronic powerlessness and passivity of the female role, and are associated with depression in women (Sturdivant, 1980:123–4).

Institutional arrangements

Structural conditions may contribute to personal problems in at least the following three ways: through material restrictions, through a lack of power or opportunity, and through conflicts between competing interest groups.

It is fairly obvious that material restrictions such as lack of resources or inappropriately allocated resources can directly cause personal inadequacy. Cases with this type of problem might include the social isolation experienced by many aged pensioners because of poor living conditions or lack of personal finances.

Undesirable personality traits can result directly from a lack of power or opportunity in a life situation. For example, manipulative behaviour such as nagging may be an attempt to exercise covert power in a powerless situation (Sturdivant, 1980:125). Seemingly 'paranoid' reactions to criticism may be the result of learning from past experience in an oppressive situation (Brodsky, 1980:57).

Conflicts between competing interest groups can be directly responsible for personal problems. For example, many family problems involving adolescent children can be analysed as conflict between the values of different generations, or between more powerful parents and their less powerful children.

Conflicts between the competing interests of a service user, worker, and social service agency can also complicate personal problems. For example, a person's problem may be exacerbated because an agreement cannot be reached with the worker or agency on the action that needs to be taken. This might be particularly the case in child protection work. Illich's treatise on the disabling aspects of the profession (1977) illustrates how the interests of client and professional are inimical to each other. Professionals need to maintain their position as the exclusive experts. They do this at the expense of clients, disabling them from becoming autonomous decision makers. The professions as a social institution then can actually further people's problems.

Social control processes

Some problems can be directly traced to attempts to oppress or exploit less powerful groups through processes of social control. Many of the ways this causes problems on behavioural, theoretical and institutional levels have just been discussed. However, a further cause of problems is the oppression and exploitation by dominant groups which needs to be added to highlight some of the more specific ways in which structural power imbalances can directly cause personal problems.

Aside from ideological restrictions, formal and informal sanctionings are among the main avenues of social control (Robertson 1977:58). Formal sanctioning, or the system of socially legalised regulations can obviously directly maintain power inequalities. For example, it has been argued that the poor are kept in poverty through social policies and economic practices that work against them (Piven & Cloward, 1971). As we noted earlier, a lack of power can be directly responsible for the problematic characteristic of some groups, and the fact that they remain powerless. Pinderhughes (1983), for example, notes that some values held by Afro-American families have developed as a clear result of powerlessness. Valuing fatalism, strength, toughness, struggle, cunning and power helps them contend with situations of racism, oppression and poverty. Unfortunately these same values can make Afro-American families vulnerable to conflict with white Americans and reluctant to accept outside assistance.

Informal sanctioning or the unwritten assumptions about correct behaviour, may also directly cause personal hardship. Undesirable attitudes and behaviour of non-conforming parties may be punished or stigmatised by dominant groups. Social ostracism or restrictions on social growth and development may result for the deviant group. The well-documented social rejection and consequent loneliness of divorcees (Hart, 1976) can be partly explained in this way.

Social labelling processes

In a similar fashion the social labelling process can contribute to personal problems by defining deviant behaviour as problematic rather than merely different. For example, Sturdivant (1980:127–8) notes that some mental illnesses such as schizophrenia in women can be associated with the non-observance of female domestic roles. Taking this together with other results, Sturdivant concludes that much of what is labelled 'schizophrenia' may be more accurately called sex-role rejection or alienation. This type of labelling is seen more clearly when considering behaviour which is acceptable for some groups but not for others; for example, the same behaviour that is seen as 'assertive' behaviour in men may be labelled as 'aggressive', and therefore problematic, in women (Sturdivant, 1980:128). In these ways negative self-perceptions and self-defeating behaviours may be caused and maintained through negative social labelling.

Social change

Social change may become a personal problem in the following ways: because of an inability to cope with social changes; or because of anachronistic personal attitudes and behaviour.

Rapid social changes may not only induce personal stress, but may cause a person to feel alienated from society and from an ability to effect change within it. (The previous chapter discussed this in some detail.) This feeling of alienation or powerlessness can be problematic because very often people need to personally change in order to keep pace with the technological and value changes that result from social change (Fook, 1984). Welfare case lists are filled with examples of people who have refused to accept changes in social mores regarding divorce, work or disability. On top of this, anachronistic attitudes and behaviour can cause conflict in peoples' lives. A classic example is that of family conflicts resulting from the 'generation gap', or conflicts between women who have accepted new ideas regarding womens' roles, and their husbands who have not. Similar problems may occur between mature-age students and uneducated peers who retain old value systems.

In this chapter I have attempted to formulate some broad guidelines to use in assessing the causes of personal problems, and the relative importance of structural and personal factors. There are always both personal and structural factors (which need to be articulated by the radical caseworker) in any problem, but their relative importance may vary and it is useful to use a continuum to help conceptualise this relative importance and the possible strategies which might be indicated. A typology of the levels at which structural factors cause personal problems, and the categories of structural causes of problems was outlined. This typology allows us to direct ourselves towards particular goals in helping individuals.

6   Goals

Now that we are clearer about how a radical caseworker might assess the causes of problems and the different categories into which a person's problems might fall, we need to focus specifically on what both the worker and person should aim for in order to help the person change the situation. In casework it is important to articulate the goal, aim or desired outcome of the worker's intervention. This not only helps to direct actions, but can also be used as a basis for evaluating the intervention to ensure that the outcome of professional help is what was intended. This, of course, is one of the hallmarks of professional accountability to the users of our services and, therefore, is obviously essential to the repertoire of the radical caseworker. Goals also 'serve as the link between the problem and the strategy' (Loewenberg, 1983:73).

In radical casework, the general aim is towards personal change, autonomy and power, gained mainly through an awareness of the influence of the social structure on the problem situation. This awareness should in turn promote the ability to control one's own life. The general goal of radical casework is similar to traditional casework in that both focus on the individual. However, while traditional casework aims to adapt personal inadequacies to deal with the environment, radical casework attempts to change aspects of the social structure which impinge on the personal life of the individual (as explained) and contribute to problems. In some senses these two goals are not mutually exclusive, since the social structure may directly cause personal inadequacy, however, whereas the

83

traditional caseworker normally limits attention to personal weaknesses or deficits within the person's immediate environment, the radical caseworker's ultimate aim is always to broaden this attention to the link between the person's problem and the social structure. In this chapter we will look at four specific radical casework goals: to decrease ideological restrictions; to decrease oppression and exploitation; to decrease the effects of social labelling; and to enable personal change and the personal ability to manage social change. These categories of goals derive from the way we have assessed, in the previous chapters, the structural causes of problems.

DECREASING IDEOLOGICAL RESTRICTIONS

I will organise discussion of these goals in terms of the different aspects of ideology outlined in chapter 5: behavioural, belief and structural restrictions.

Behavioural restrictions

The goal of decreasing the behavioural restrictions on individual people mainly involves loosening the strict social-role distinctions which confine individual behaviour or draw rigid lines between the behaviour of different individuals. There are five specific aspects to this main goal: broadening role possibilities; resolving social-role conflicts; developing alternative roles; changing roles; and increasing awareness of role socialisation.

1 Role possibilities may be broadened by aiming to increase the range and variety of behaviour that is acceptable in a particular chosen role. For example, someone who is feeling stressed because of being stuck in a breadwinning role may be encouraged to reduce the stress by sharing the financial responsibility with other household members and taking turns on some of the responsibilities for home maintenance.

2 Conflicts between social roles may be resolved in a similar way by broadening a role to successfully incorporate other (seemingly conflicting) aspects. Clarifying behavioural choices and deciding whether these really are contradictory, or whether they may be accommodated through new arrangements may be necessary. If, for example, a mother wants to pursue a career outside the home but feels some guilt from the apparent conflict between roles, one way to resolve the conflict might be to clarify the

behaviours actually necessary for the performance of each role, and then to work out a program whereby conflicting behaviours can be juggled. The same goal can be pursued if there is conflict between two people over the performance of the same role. As with our example of the breadwinner, role conflicts may be reduced between people if they can be persuaded to share or jointly perform some of the particular behaviours necessary to the role.

3 Alternative roles may be developed by creating new role possibilities. An unhappily retired professional person, for example, need not necessarily give up the professional stimulation and input normally associated with an active career but may develop a new role as a voluntary consultant.

4 Existing roles may actually be changed. This is an area in which the feminist movement has made a great deal of progress. Roles which have been traditionally seen as male or female, with an assumption of corresponding characteristics, are now being challenged. It is now generally accepted that women do not have to be submissive, and men do not have to be aggressive. In the workplace it is now becoming recognised that managers may be successful using traditionally female characteristics such as interpersonal skills, rather than a necessary hard-nosed male approach. It is conceivable that the traditional housewife and complementary breadwinner roles may not exist in the long-term future. Individuals may also opt not to continue playing a particular role if they decide it is problematic for them. For example, a person who is unhappy in the workplace because of a belief that distasteful games must played in order to be successful, may simply decide that the conforming game will not be played any longer. This might typically be the case for low status employees expected (without formal recognition) to perform the tasks of senior staff in order to preserve their position.

5 By aiming to increase awareness of role socialisation the social worker and client may work to change problematic behaviour which is associated with certain roles. Overly dependent, chronically ill people, for example, who are causing problems for their families may be shown how the dependent behaviour associated with their role may not apply to all activities. They may need assistance with housekeeping and lawn mowing, but not with decision making. They may be shown that the secondary gain from playing a particular role may be achieved in other less dependent ways.

Decreasing belief restrictions

As we have already established, people often hold beliefs or assumptions which restrict their behaviour and confine them to socially defined roles. Sometimes the person and worker may need to aim at weakening the hold of these beliefs in the person's life. There are three specific aspects to attaining this goal: the challenging of false beliefs; resolving or tolerating conflicting beliefs; and modifying self-defeating beliefs.

1   It may be important for a person to challenge false beliefs because believing them actually serves groups powerful within the existing social system, rather than the individual person. In this sense what needs to be challenged is the function the false idea serves, rather than its inherent truth or falsity. However, there may be some cases where the belief is demonstrably false, and only supports misguided behaviour. For example, the belief that women are 'nothing' without men was a common misconception among some women seeking counselling (Russianoff, 1982). In these cases the help might aim at challenging this view, noting the personal worth of each woman, and also exposing how believing this idea ensures that women will restrict themselves to roles which require the presence of a man.
2   If a problem is caused by the fact that people hold conflicting beliefs about their social world, the aim may be to resolve or learn to tolerate the conflict. In a radical approach, conflict is not necessarily assumed to be a negative thing. It may be simply the belief that conflict is negative which causes the situation to be problematic. Reframing the situation, and seeing conflict as a natural and normal or expected aspect of social life may be appropriate. If individuals decide, however, that they would prefer to resolve the conflict, this may be achieved by examining the actual choices involved in the conflict, and locating the sources of the conflict extraneous to the person. For example, conflict between different cultural beliefs is often a problem for migrant parents and the first generation of children raised in the adopted country. If the situation can be reframed so that it is seen as a problem arising simply from the need to settle in a new environment, parents and children may feel less antagonism towards each other and the conflict between them may be lessened as they together try to forge new ways of thinking and acting which will allow them to cope with the changes wrought by their move.
3   Some social beliefs held by people may be clearly self-defeating, as with the women referred to earlier who believed they were

worthless without a male companion. By simply aiming to focus on and modify any attitudes like this which are obviously self-defeating, particularly any attitudes of self-blame, low-esteem or poor self-image, or beliefs of personal powerlessness, the radical caseworker may then show how these can arise from structural conditions, and help the person construct more self-empowering personal values. A depressed woman who is primarily engaged in home duties may believe, for example, that she is not intelligent or capable of anything else; the caseworker may aim to show her that this belief may simply be a result of the fact that she has little social interaction and therefore little intellectual stimulation. She may then learn to re-evaluate her personal strengths in the light of what she might be capable of, given the right opportunities and experiences.

Decreasing structural restrictions

The very real structures which restrict personal autonomy and power may be weakened in three main ways: redistribution or provision of material resources; increasing power and access to resources or opportunities; and redistributing or equalising power between competing interest groups.

1   Actually providing, redistributing or rearranging material resources is the most obvious way to decrease the material aspect of structural restrictions imposed on disadvantaged people. For example, providing child care facilities may allow a mother to undertake tertiary study.

    In many instances, however, the injection of new resources into clients' situations may not be needed. It may simply be an issue of rearranging what resources they already have at their disposal, or redistributing the resources from other people in their lives. Let me illustrate with an example of a young man with a physical disability who would like to live independently away from his parents but believes he cannot manage financially: by combining his assets and pension with several other people and setting up joint accommodation with them he may be able to do so.

2   Increasing power over or access to resources or opportunities is another important way to foster personal autonomy. There may be several ways in which this can be achieved. Sometimes simply clarifying the process involved in obtaining resources may be sufficient. Sometimes relevant information may need to be provided. In some instances actually aiming to first weaken the self-defeating beliefs and behaviours associated with the

powerlessness may be enough to allow the person to create and act upon opportunities. This is commonly termed a 'goal of empowerment' by many writers (Pinderhughes, 1983; Furlong, 1987). We will deal with the specific strategies and techniques of empowerment in the final chapter.

3   Redistributing or equalising power between competing interest groups in the person's life is another goal which may help to lessen structural restrictions. If the person is a member of a social group which is traditionally less powerful and in conflict with another, it may be useful to aim to equalise the power imbalance between the two groups. For instance, in a family conflict between parents and teenage children, the radical case-worker could aim to redistribute some parental power to the teenagers by increasing the decision-making input of the ado-lescents. This may not only resolve the conflict between the two groups and hopefully improve the situation for all involved, but it will also empower individual adolescents.

DECREASING OPPRESSION AND EXPLOITATION

One major way in which a radical caseworker can decrease the oppression and exploitation of individual people is by aiming to decrease their specific effects on individuals. We have discussed some of these particular goals already, such as the aim to modify self-defeating behaviour or attitudes. Another goal would be to develop personal power. Another, more socially oriented goal might be to create or link up with alternative support or status systems for a person whose socially self-defeating beliefs are unshakeable. Many support and lobby groups can provide this type of alternative social identity. For example, parents of a person with an intellectual disability may achieve some social recognition (which may be socially therapeutic for them) through involvement in relevant com-munity work to bring about better resourcing of services for people with disabilities.

DECREASING THE EFFECTS OF SOCIAL LABELLING

The first logical step involved in decreasing the effects of any social labelling in the person's life is to increase awareness of the ways she or he may be socially labelled. This may help to shift the blame for problems from any characteristics which are personally inherent to the surrounding social attitudes which label those characteris-tics as undesirable, and create the conditions which mean that having these characteristics is a social disadvantage. In this way, one of the effects of social labelling, the attitude of self-blame, is reduced.

Another goal which is associated with decreasing social labelling is to increase the individual's choices about social-role options, similar to the 'third' goal we mentioned under 'Decreasing ideological restrictions' in this chapter. One of the ways this can be done is to increase people's understanding of behaviour or attitudes which may not be socially acceptable in given situations. People are then freer to make clearer choices about their own lifestyle, which they might personally desire, even though it is negatively socially labelled. Sturdivant's (1980:127–8) argument, which we discussed in the previous chapter, that some schizophrenia in women should be more correctly labelled 'sex-role rejection', illustrates this perfectly. It is also less personally demoralising to have chosen to reject a socially expected sex role, than to be 'mentally ill'.

ENABLING PERSONAL CHANGE

Personal change is a goal which should be aimed for simply because the personally inhibiting effects of structural problems may need to be changed. Also it is often necessary for people to change in order to cope with social changes in their own lives. This goal is also associated with the goal of gaining power and control over one's life. The fostering of self-acceptance, the encouragement of flexible attitudes towards conflict and change are also part of this. As an example, strongly religious people may cope better with their own marriage break-up if they can see how they have changed since the beginning of their marriage, and how old beliefs and customs may not be appropriate to their present life needs.

An awareness of historical context can achieve two purposes. First, it can help the person accept historical and cultural influences and the effect of changes in these. A corresponding view, that values and customs change over time, develops a more flexible attitude to changeable situations. For example, family generation gap conflicts may be partly resolved if the parents can see how their own attitudes may have changed since their own youth, as will their children's attitudes change over time in the future.

Secondly, feelings of social alienation may be decreased through an awareness of historical context. If people can see how they are partly a product of their times, and that current times are both a product of the past and will be an influence on the future, a sense of personal power or importance may be encouraged. This may be particularly useful with old people, who may feel, perhaps, that their lives, now drawing to a close, have been unimportant. The worker may be able to instil a sense of the breadth of historical changes these people have experienced, and how all they have seen will contribute to the future.

7 Strategies and techniques

In the previous chapters I have traced how assessment criteria and goals for radical casework action can be directly derived from the theoretical assumptions we make about how the social structure influences individual experience. In this chapter I will identify particular strategies and techniques which are developed from these assumptions, and which will help achieve radical casework goals.

Chapter 2 made clear that although radical casework is different from traditional casework, they are alike in many ways. Often the same skills may be used in both a traditional and/or radical manner, depending on the overall purpose of the casework encounter. It is the goals rather than the skills that are different. Interpersonal and communication skills, for example, may be used by a worker to either help clients accept their own inadequacies, or to identify structural causes of their problems. However, a caseworker with basically radical goals may have to modify, transform, or even create new techniques to achieve radical goals.

It is some of these changed or new types of strategies that I will focus on, having assumed that a competence in basic interpersonal and other casework skills (traditionally practised by caseworkers) is also necessary. You should, therefore, use the techniques discussed in this chapter as an *extension* of traditional strategies, rather than a *substitute* for them.

STRATEGIES FOR BUREAUCRACY

It is important to discuss the strategies for coping with the bureaucracy of casework practice first, since much (in some cases most) social work action occurs outside the one-to-one interview situation with the client, often in a bureaucratic agency setting. Most caseworkers are also employees often in highly bureaucratic environments, and it is often these environments which will determine and define what the caseworker and client can or cannot do. In order to help the particular casework client, the focus of change may have to be the agency or bureaucracy.

Documentation and research

For the radical caseworker, the importance of documenting and researching what we do cannot be underestimated. Public knowledge of the types of problems individuals may experience, and responses to their experiences of the social structure are invaluable in making social policies responsive to individual needs. Radical research can support radical practice similar to the ways in which conventional research supports conventional practice. Research and documentation are also necessary to help develop radical analysis and practice, always an ongoing concern. They help to make the radical ideas more socially visible, and increase the possibility of their acceptance and adoption. Research should also be made more radical by increasing accessibility to it, thus encouraging maximum participation (Galper, 1980: 213–15). From a feminist point of view, research should as far as possible maintain the equality of those researched with those doing the research and for whom the research is done (Roberts, 1981:26).

Analysis of agency policy and procedure

An analysis of agency procedure may reveal policies that support social inequalities. Where possible, agency procedures regarding intake, obtaining appointment times, and referral, or policies about opening hours, access and eligibility for help should maximise equality and power sharing with clients. For example, the caseworker may need to initiate or support endeavours to make services as accessible as possible, such as client self-referral, or the elimination of overly long waiting lists. Similarly, information about the benefits of a service should be freely available.

An analysis of the formal and informal system of reward and punishment within an agency bureaucracy can bring to notice repressive policies and practices which may need to be changed to benefit the client. An example will illustrate this point. It is the rule in a certain sheltered workshop that employees can only see the caseworker when the workshop manager refers them there for misbehaviour. This is a classic instance of casework being used as 'social control'; that is, seeking casework help is perceived as a sanction, or form of punishment for wrongdoing, and as such is incorporated into the system of control in the workshop. In this type of setting, the radical caseworker may need to show how boring work, overly authoritarian managers, or perhaps the frustration of being socially labelled as 'developmentally disabled' can contribute to 'misbehaviour'. The caseworker may set up procedures for employees to be referred for different reasons, such as when they themselves choose.

Occupational tactics

These refer to strategies for opposing oppressive bureaucratic policies and can be implemented immediately in most work settings, before more structural changes have taken place. Thus part of their value is that they begin in the workplace of conventional casework. The technique of 'client refusal' has been widely suggested as useful in this way (Simpkin, 1983:181; Cohen, 1975:87). This involves a caseworker refusing to accept the client as 'case', but rather as a potential 'political ally' in need of protection and care. For example, caseworkers may oppose psychotherapeutic treatment of clients if their problems are primarily structurally caused.

Case conferences or staff meetings may be the arenas where this is achieved. Agency case assessment and intake categories may need to be revised to include cases of primarily material or structural deprivation. Simpkin quotes an instance of social workers refusing to receive children into care solely because their parents were homeless (1979:155). They were rejecting the implication that the problem was solely that of the children. The role of political ally in instances like these involves the caseworker demonstrating that any refusal to help people in conventional terms is being done on political grounds. The aim is to expose any political inequalities and divisions in welfare help (Cohen, 1975:89).

A range of other oppositional tactics have been suggested by the London–Edinburgh Weekend Return Group (1980:92–101). They include attempts to overcome bureaucratic tendencies to individualise clients' problems, and to reject any bureaucratic categories that may support this. (These are similar to client refusal.) They also suggest that caseworkers and clients can define themselves in class terms, focusing on issues of power, rights and decision making. As well, problems can be defined in the way that clients and workers choose, rather than in bureaucratic terms. Clients of Social Security, for example, may prefer to be seen as 'fixed-income earners', rather than 'pensioners' or 'beneficiaries'. Creating new roles outside the official brief is also suggested as a way of refusing bureaucratic procedure. In a similar way, rejecting managerial priorities, and establishing alternative worker and client priorities, can help achieve this. Another way might be to establish alternative decision-making structures within the bureaucracy, such as caseworkers forming their own groups to make recommendations to management.

'The unfinished'

Mathieson's concept of 'the unfinished' is a useful stance to assume in relation to short-term achievements (Cohen, 1975:89). 'The unfinished' is basically an approach which views small achievements as legitimate as long as they are kept open to change, and are continually viewed as being part of larger scale political changes. Changes effected at agency level by radical caseworkers may be usefully viewed in this light. Although 'the unfinished' denotes an attitude more than a specific technique, it does indicate certain action strategies. For example, caseworkers should continually justify and explain, to both co-workers and clients, the larger scale purpose of any smaller changes. Any minor changes should be monitored and modified or extended if necessary. If a specific change is not successful, and traditional practices must be re-instated, this should not be regarded as a failure, or as an indication that radical changes are not possible per se. The longer term goal should always be kept in mind, and the information gained from momentary setback used in the continuing effort.

Political tactics

Techniques that involve direct struggles for power may be necessary when conventional avenues for negotiation or resolution have broken down, and an unjust or 'unethical' situation prevails (Goldberg & Elliot, 1980: 480). The caseworker may be seeking to change the situation for a particular client, or to generally modify agency policy.

When confronting power holders who are resistant to change, the technique of polarising (as per Hain, 1975:121) may be useful. By reducing the argument to its essential differences and presenting the case in black and white terms, the radical caseworker allows the ideological split to express itself fully. In the stark contrast of the two views, the power holders may feel presented in a bad light, and make some shift accordingly.

Goldberg and Elliot (1980:481–3) note a number of other tactics to help obtain compliance from power holders, First, the perceptions of power holders can be manipulated so that, for example, they are over-sensitised to a particular issue by radical caseworkers continually drawing attention to it in a variety of ways. As well, prolonging and reinforcing doubt about power holders' judgement may make them change. Secondly, radical caseworkers should consider the well-known 'lesser of the two evils routine' of suggesting an extreme position, so that in the subsequent bargaining and compromise, the more modest measure (which may have been the originally intended objective) is obtained.

The many rules for radical tactics discussed by Alinsky (1971:125–64) may also be modified for use by caseworkers in agency settings. For example, opposition can be worn down by a technique of simply keeping the pressure on, and operations should be developed to maintain it. Caseworkers may oppose an agency rule of not allowing clients into the tearoom. They could continually raise the issue at staff meetings and during informal discussions. Workers could persist in taking each of their own clients in the tearoom for a few minutes of each session for a preliminary cup of coffee. Colleagues from other agencies may be primed to ask 'innocent' questions about whether clients are allowed in the tearoom.

Occupational survival

Although radical caseworkers are not unique in their potential to suffer burn out (excessive stress, depression and fatigue often associated with work in the helping professions; see Gambrill, (1983:403)), there may be particularly radical ways of dealing with it. Foremost among these would be an attempt to work collectively with colleagues (Corrigan & Leonard, 1978:155). This not only provides social and emotional support for individual workers, but also acts as a basis for organised change within an agency. Such teamwork with co-workers can have its own consciousness-raising effects, and associated benefits like encouraging reflective action.

Radical caseworkers may also need to learn how to deal with conflict and isolation on a personal basis, since many of these radical practices may well bring about tension and distance between them and their colleagues who may be in disagreement with them.

DEVELOPING CRITICAL AWARENESS

Skills to develop critical awareness are basically derived from techniques associated with the processes of conscientisation and consciousness-raising. Both of these processes are essentially educational in that they involve becoming more aware about the social world (Leonard, 1975:59). They are particularly important in radical casework for two reasons: first, they emphasise liberating the individual from social and political oppression; secondly, they place importance on being conscious of the structural conditions which cause personal problems.

Some social workers have questioned the uncritical adoption of conscientisation as a social work strategy, because they argue that it is really about politicising clients, not necessarily about helping them, and that all social work, radical or conventional, is primarily about helping people regardless of political persuasion (Bailey & Brake, 1980:60). This is not to say that social work practice—traditional or radical—is not political; only the type of politics and the degree to which it is articulated vary. However, we may need to modify such techniques to ensure that the politicisation which occurs is therapeutic. For example, consciousness-raising groups often have secondary psychotherapeutic effects on their members (Brodsky, 1980).

The concept of conscientisation originates largely from the work of Friere, and refers to 'learning to perceive social, political and economic contradictions, and to take action against the oppressive elements of reality' (1972:15). There is, thus, both an awareness element as well as an action element in the concept. Freire contrasts the conscientisation approach to education with traditional education's 'banking' model which he claims can obstruct the development of a conscientised awareness. In the 'banking' model knowledge is stored up, as if in a bank, thus denying that education and knowledge are actually processes of inquiry, rather than merely a store of information. Furthermore, in this type of approach, the educators behave as if knowledge is a gift which they (the knowledgeable) bestow upon others (the knowledgeless), whom they assume are in absolute ignorance. This is part of an ideology which perpetuates oppression by the more powerful over the less powerful (Freire, 1972:46). In addition, this type of education can further oppress in that it precludes people from being able to act independently (Alfrero, 1972:74–5), since they must always obtain their education from outside themselves.

Alfrero traces the process of conscientisation in three stages (1972:75–6). The first stage—or state—is a magical consciousness, a fatalistic type of consciousness which accepts 'facts' dominating one's life from outside. Therefore, individual action is impossible, and one can only meekly submit to situations that already exist. The second stage is of naive consciousness, an awareness of being able to dominate the 'facts' from outside, and, therefore, being free to understand them. The third stage is of critical consciousness, an awareness of 'facts', and their causal relationship to social circumstances. This requires an ability to both observe and analyse reality; that is, an active consciousness.

The goal of the caseworker in helping to conscientise a person is, thus, to attain this third stage of development: a critical awareness which allows the person to see the situation objectively, understand what causes it and work out what to do about it. In helping clients attain this critical awareness, the caseworker needs to refer to some of the concepts discussed earlier. From these, the following techniques emerge.

Separating internal from the external

The main differentiation that needs to be made in separating the sources of experiences and expectations is between experience or situations that exist because that is what a client personally desires, and experiences or situations that exist in their life because that is what is socially desirable (Gilbert, 1980:248). This is similar to making the distinction in feminist terms mentioned earlier between the institution (aspects of a person's experience which are brought about by a patriarchal system) and the experience (subjective aspects of the experience, which are independent of patriarchal influence) (Eisenstein, 1984:70).

Of course, some situations may involve elements of both. For example, a woman may be a mother both because she personally enjoys children and because she also thinks it is socially expected of her. In such a case it may be helpful for her to understand which is the most important reason, or which aspects of mothering she does because she personally chooses, and which she performs because of social pressure. It may be that she reads to her children every night before bed because she personally feels that is an important part of mothering but she refrains from paid employment outside the home because she is afraid that other people will think her a bad mother. In this case helping her see what she does because she so chooses and what she does for 'outside' reasons will help her develop a critical awareness about her situation, and thus give her a basis for deciding which aspects she can and will change if she so desires.

In helping people differentiate internal (personal) and external (social) aspects of their experience it may be helpful to break down experiences by: listing 'who benefits'; clarifying the reasons for certain situations; searching for conflicts and then contrasting social expectations with psychological needs or personal choices; or asking the person to imagine hypothetical ideal situations which may then expose any hidden personal desires.

Critical questioning

Critical questioning is a form of questioning which may also help clients separate the internal from the external. It is often used by feminist therapists as a crucial technique to foster critical responses to social expectations (Thomas, 1977:451–3). The strategy involves the worker asking questions which might expose any of the person's stereotyped or socially conditioned assumptions. The difference between normal questioning and critical questioning goes as follows: in response to a woman who says, 'I should give my family more attention', the worker might normally ask, 'Why do you think that?' Such a question can imply that there is one clear-cut answer, and may prompt the woman to give the one which is closest to being 'off the top of her head', such as 'My kids told me so'.

On the other hand, critical questioning can show that there might be a number of answers, or that there may be personal or social conflicts involved in the situation. For example, a critical questioner might respond to the same woman, 'Is that what you think, or what you think is expected of you?' The woman is then more likely to consider possible conflicts in the situation, responding, for example, 'It's both, but I want to do what is expected of me. Don't you think that's right?'

The worker is thus presented with an opportunity to explore the woman's perceptions of her expectations and how she feels she must act in relation to them. This will also give her a basis from which to understand to what extent her life may represent her own personal choices on the one hand or social conditioning (and her beliefs about it) on the other. In the longer term this may give her a basis for more control over her life through an increased critical awareness of how external factors may have not only determined her life in the past, but may be continuing to do so in the present.

Challenging false myths and restricted role behaviours

As well as exposing the role of external factors in determining life experience through critical questioning, there may be a need to actually focus on particular beliefs (which may function as myths for the person) and undesirable stereotyped behaviours which are highlighted in the process. While the subjective perception of the person must always be respected, it is sometimes necessary to challenge some of the beliefs or behaviours that contribute to the problem situation. This can be done in a number of ways. Through discussion or demonstration people can be shown how their ideas about what is desirable (their values) and about what is possible naturally determine what they will (or will not) attempt, thus partly determining the roles they play in life. I will illustrate with a detailed example. Some people may hold negative beliefs that those who engage in tertiary education are 'professional students'. As a result they themselves may scorn education and thus miss out on any social opportunities afforded by it. In this case the belief about 'professional students' needs closer examination—what do these people believe about tertiary education? Where do those beliefs come from? What do they think about people who study at higher levels? Would they be like this if they attempted study themselves? Is this what is preventing them from attempting further study?—and so on. This type of discussion will provide the worker with the opportunity to help clients link their restricted behaviour with particular beliefs about classes of other people, to whom they feel they don't belong, and demonstrate that they may need to change their beliefs in order to give them more freedom to act in other ways.

Other types of behaviour may need to be challenged by showing how they can cause people to be labelled in a certain way, thus robbing them of the confidence or inclination to change the role. For example, a mother who is overly nurturant may become disinclined to assert her own needs. Her behaviour may be socially interpreted as 'boring', she may begin to see herself this way and, therefore, lose the ability to behave any differently. While much of this problem situation is caused by the fatuous assumptions of other people, it is important, in developing critical awareness, that this person can also clearly see the role of her own behaviour in contributing to such a situation. There is then a clear immediate focus for action—she may, for example, decide to begin articulating her own wishes, or she may actively challenge the false assumptions of others.

On a more concrete level, a belief may simply have to be exposed and challenged as having little proven basis or in some cases as being completely false. The idea that there is a Mr Right for every woman, or that poor people are that way because they are lazy, are two such examples. In other cases, a belief may need to be analysed, showing the aspects that are empirically based, those that are not, and those that are held chiefly because they perform primarily ideological functions. For example, the belief that women are better at domestic duties than men probably has some empirical validity, as women are more practised at housework (because of social conditioning). The belief that women are inherently better at house-work probably has less validity, since men, once trained, appear to be equally capable around the house. This view, however, also performs ideological functions in that it can serve as an excuse for men not to attempt housework and to keep women in the home. Once clients become aware which of their ideas are valid (and why), and which primarily restrict their behaviour, they are in a better position to broaden their role choices.

Creating alternatives

Helping people simply conceive then create alternatives to their situation is another way to develop critical awareness. In a sense a worker is here attempting to help a client imagine the outcome of a situation reviewed critically then changed. There is thus a basis for comparison with the present situation, and it is easier to imagine ways to change it.

One of the techniques suggested for use in consciousness-raising groups, the 'creative solutions rap group' (Kirk, 1983: 181–3) provides an example of this. The group begins by exploring the concerns of the members; 'brainstorming' in order to imagine a society without the conditions that caused these personal concerns follows, then the group refocuses on the original problems. In this way, new options may be discovered.

Although consciousness-raising is essentially a group process (Longres & McLeod, 1980:273), some of the techniques may be modified for use in casework.

Both the worker and client together can speculate imaginatively about a situation in which the client's problems do not exist. These new conceptions can then be examined in the light of the person's present personal circumstances. Depressed people, for example, might describe their situation as involving boring work, few friends and inattentive family. In picturing a life without these restraints, they may see themselves as changing jobs, taking up part-time study or a hobby, and organising family get-togethers. Each of these possibilities might then be examined for immediate feasibility, and the steps to achieve it examined.

Picturing an option is not, of course, the same as achieving it. But the imaginative exercise may, at the very least, help break down any attitudinal or mental barriers to attempting it. More than that, the exercise may be the beginning of teaching the person to create choices and alternatives for themselves through a thoughtful rehearsal of the experience prior to actually attempting it.

ADVOCACY

Advocacy was one of the earliest suggestions as an appropriate role for radical caseworkers (Terrell, 1973). The role of advocate is as one who acts for, mediates or intercedes for another (Stuart, 1976). Such a role is in keeping with the 'welfare rights' aspects of a radical approach which seek to ensure that welfare recipients are accorded their rightful resources and entitlements. Taking an advocacy role also implies less blaming of the victim, since the client is seen as a person to be protected, rather than a problem to be solved. There are some limitations to the practice of advocacy, such as social and bureaucratic restrictions, or competing rightful claims (Stuart, 1976:163). However, advocacy can still be employed even in a limited way by the caseworker.

Particular strategies may be employed to ensure that casework clients receive full and proper use of social services; in other words, to ensure that social welfare services are as responsive as possible to individual client needs. The bulk of these strategies may take place outside the casework interview setting. Specific bureaucratic techniques to effect changes in policy were discussed at the beginning of this chapter. Other specific strategies might simply be to provide clients with full information about their entitlements and the wherewithal to obtain them. Finding loopholes in bureaucratic rules, or bending rules or situations to suit the client may also be essential (Thorpe, 1981).

For a caseworker to be an effective advocate, a full and intimate knowledge of both formal and informal agency rules and procedures is needed (The Ad Hoc Committee on Advocacy, 1969). This familiarity may need to extend to any agency with which the caseworker deals. For example, the worker may need to know the official rules as formally stated, and as they apply in practice. If there are discrepancies, there may be loopholes discovered in the gap. Knowledge of the personalities of bureaucratic staff and interpersonal relationships can indicate further possible loopholes in agency procedure; if caseworkers know, for example, that a certain Social Security clerk feels sympathetic towards single mothers perhaps they should arrange for their single mother clients to be assessed for benefits by that particular staff member.

Coupled with a competent knowledge of agency procedure, effective advocacy requires expertise in multiple interpersonal skills. Outside the agency setting, the caseworker may need to act as an advocate for clients in, for example, their social environment, such as interceding with family members to reduce pressure on a client, or representing and arguing a client's case to the referring bureaucracy.

Skills in handling conflict are invaluable in situations like these. Negotiating and bargaining skills may be necessary when interceding in the client's environment. Loewenberg notes several skills (1983:309): bringing parties together to negotiate terms; defining the situation so that negotiating and bargaining can occur; or acting as trainer or consultant to the client.

EMPOWERMENT

Empowerment refers to techniques that aim at sharing with, or giving clients power (Loewenberg, 1983: 319–20). They are based on the radical social work assumption that many personal problems are caused by lack of power or by power inequalities. They are congruent with the goals of helping people gain power and autonomy in their lives.

The technique of making power explicit is useful to help equalise the client–worker relationship. This may involve an analysis of the client's life as well as the present casework situation, concentrating on the realities and perceptions of power. The worker may need to refuse to accept clients' potential power, and to focus the responsibility for change on them. On a more specific level, the caseworker may need to ensure that a client is aware of every decision made and the reasons for the choice. Although some choices may be limited by social or personal restrictions, the client may still need by be aware of the process of exercising choice within these, and thus may learn to separate personal responsibility from social restriction.

A second technique is simply one of giving clients powerful experiences, or experiences in which they act in a more than usually powerful role. Pinderhughes (1983:336) quotes the example of a middle-aged woman client apparently resistant to change, who finally trusted a worker enough to expose her vulnerabilities, which were one of the reasons for her apparent resistance. This was partly achieved after several encounters in which the client, who was good at sewing, taught the worker to sew. In this case, experiencing the ability to share power in a teaching role may have made the woman feel safer with the worker. This example suggests many possibilities, since it is often the case that clients have skills or knowledge which they can offer to the caseworker or others. Voluntary work can be used well to this effect.

As well, giving clients powerful experiences can also have the effect of sensitising them to potential power in their lives. It may also give them an arena in which to practise 'powerful behaviour' for other areas of their life. For example, the woman cited above may have been encouraged to be more assertive about her own needs after she had become used to demonstrating her expertise at sewing.

An empowerment perspective can be applied in supporting clients' efforts to change their social world. In this way clients and social workers may see their actions in political, rather than sole interpersonal terms. Radical casework help can also involve learning skills in creating alliances; building coalitions; overcoming organisational barriers or engaging in political action on behalf of or with individual clients (Pinderhughes, 1983:334). The traditional techniques of utilising and fostering interpersonal social support networks may be re-conceived in these more political terms.

THE CASEWORK RELATIONSHIP

The casework relationship is included here, not necessarily because it is a concrete skill, but because it is traditionally viewed by caseworkers as an essential means of helping the client (Biestek, 1957; Tilbury, 1977:166–72). The experience of trust and care that may develop between client and worker is seen as a valuable tool. The acceptance experienced by the client can provide a safe environment within which to recognise any psychological defences and learn to cope without them.

The main difference between a traditional and a radical casework relationship is that the latter places emphasis on equality and sharing, rather than the often unbalanced paternalistic style of many traditional workers. Equality in the relationship can be emphasised in a number of ways. Making the worker's skills, values and assumptions explicit in order to share them and make them accessible for debate is one way. Contracts (Compton & Galaway, 1989:471–3) can be used to similar effect. Focusing on the client's potential power in the immediate situation, and refusing to accept responsibility for that power is suggested by some feminist therapists (for example, Thomas, 1977:450). Simply acknowledging and discussing unavoidable power imbalances may be an easy starting place. Refusing to professionally interpret clients' conversation, but rather airing and checking out 'hunches' or 'feelings' with them is less interpersonally distancing. In this sense, the radical casework and client relationship is best seen as one of joint learning through an exchange of impressions, rather than an imposition of one person's interpretations on another.

What many of these suggestions have in common, apart from striving to equalise the relationship, is the associated role of reducing the social and interpersonal distancing so often caused by playing the professional role. Another obvious way of doing this is minimising the use of jargon, or avoiding lengthy explanations of esoteric theory. Although there are elaborate theories which explain structural influences on the individual, these are experienced in concrete and specific ways at the individual level. The caseworker needs to have a working familiarity with the precise ways in which individual clients are affected by the broad socio-economic structure. As social work professionals we have developed colloquial ways to speak about psychological aspects of our own and our clients' lives. We need to do the same when speaking about structural influences. For example, instead of speaking about 'patriarchy', we can speak about 'male-dominated society'. Instead of speaking about 'ideology' we can speak about 'socially conditioned ideas'.

Professional distancing can also be reduced by an increased use of self in the relationship. Appropriate self-disclosure, and sharing of positive and negative experiences serve to make the worker more of a normal person rather than a distant professional (Thomas, 1977:451). A similar idea is behind that of the dialogical relationship, in which perceptions of the social world are shared in order to conscientise clients to the structural aspects of their problem (Leonard, 1875:59). This concept was discussed in detail earlier in this chapter under 'Developing critical awareness'.

Interviewing techniques

The radical goals of encouraging client autonomy and lessening oppression and exploitation indicate that principles of equality and sharing are important. These can be furthered in the following ways in different aspects of the interview.

Physical setting of the interview

The physical setting of the interview should be designed to minimise status distinctions between client and worker, and to encourage maximum sharing and co-operation. For example, an office environment decorated as informally as possible, with some personal touches, may help indicate that the caseworker is a 'person' who can hold an unthreatening conversation, rather than a more faceless 'official' of higher authority than the client. Similarly, 'interviews' conducted while doing the supermarket shopping or doing the washing up (particularly relevant if client and worker are both women), giving the other a lift somewhere, or over lunch in the park, provide a setting to equalise roles, and help break down the mystique of the 'professional' interview.

Appropriate structuring of the interview process

If the interview is conducted in a normal office setting, the interview can still be structured to minimise status distinctions between the two participants. For example, meeting people to be interviewed in the reception area, rather than having them ushered into your office, helps establish more equal rapport.

In a similar fashion, making sure adequate introductions on *both* sides are performed, helps establish equality. Clients should be told exactly who workers are, why their case has been assigned to them in particular and so on. Such information may help clients feel some control over the situation, or at least give them the opportunity to negotiate for appropriate help. Some feminist therapists extend this idea by encouraging their clients to 'shop around' or exercise consumer rights in finding appropriate help. This, of course, may be limited (for example, in rural areas), or most relevant in areas where there is a large number of private practitioners. Nevertheless, this type of attitude can at least help to keep clients informed, demystify the therapist role (Gilbert, 1980:249) and help to maximise professional accountability.

Formulating agreements or contracts between worker and client has become widely advocated in social work (for example, Pincus & Minahan, 1973). This can be done in an informal and preliminary way simply by making the worker's and client's assumptions and expectations about help clear right from the beginning. On a basic level it aids communication, but is also a way of sharing power with the client by giving an early opportunity for negotiation. An example of this might be when someone, such as a retired headmaster, seeks help from a young female caseworker. Since he is used to being in a position of authority over young people, he may harbour some uncertainties about her youth or competence to deal with his situation. He should then be encouraged to air any doubts; these should be discussed, and the caseworker's perceptions about helping the headmaster also aired. If an acceptable understanding cannot be reached (which is probably unlikely if there has been give and take on both sides), the man can be informed of his options for alternative help in this situation.

Access to the interview

Equality and sharing can be encouraged by maximising client access to interviews with caseworkers. For this reason, formalities such as lengthy waiting lists or overly bureaucratic referral procedures should be minimised. Practices like dropping in, or not requiring formal appointment times may be preferred. Where possible, clients should be encouraged to nominate the time and place of the interview.

Similarly, clients should not be kept waiting for unduly long periods without explanation or forewarning.

Strategies for collecting information

Like the traditional caseworker, the radical caseworker will need information about the client's social situation in order to help assess the situation and decide what can be done about it. Interpersonal skills which are sensitive to and show respect for the private nature of much of the information (and the person's right to withhold it, or at least know why it is required) are necessary to a radical approach. Often a simple acknowledgement of privacy and an explanation of how information will help the worker and client will suffice. This also means that the worker must be accountable to the client; that is, must be able to justify the need for private information. The information elicited must be relevant to the problem for which the person is seeking help. This discourages needless prying for its own sake, under the mistaken impression that the professional caseworker needs to know all about the client before she or he can help.

Caseworkers have been taught traditionally to be mindful of a number of aspects of the client's social situation. Sometimes compiling a list of facts about the person's social situation can help organise the caseworker's thinking. Such lists might include family relationships, housing, financial position, employment, education, social group membership, religion, and the involvement of medical and social institutions (Hollis, 1964:179–80). A radical caseworker would extend the list to include facets of the person's social life which reflect the influences of the broader social structure. The following list is a helpful way of organising the information at hand in order to guide the worker's and client's understanding of the situation:

- any socially originated values or 'myths' held by the person; how strongly they are held; how they affect the person's life
- evidence of interpersonal, ideological or social conflict in the person's life, such as from contrary expectations from perceived social pressures, or pressures from significant others in the person's life
- any membership of social groups particularly minority or deviant groups which might attract social labelling
- sources of power in the person's life, particularly any power vested within the person, but also that exercised by institutional authorities or by significant others
- sources and types of decision making in the person's life: who makes

the important life decisions? How are they made? In what ways does the person participate in these?

- social class of the person; how the related sub-cultural values and material position of that class affects the person's life
- gender of the person; how the related subcultural values and material position of this affects her or his life
- age or historical position of the person; how the related subcultural values and the material position of this affects her or his life
- the person's perception of control in life; how much is had; whether it's felt any change can be effected in life or the environment
- any social roles played by the person, particularly gender-related roles; how rigidly are they adhered to; what significant others are dependent upon or reinforce them; whether the person feels bound by them
- any social labels attached to the person, particularly strongly negative or positive ones which determine behaviour
- any contact with social authorities or institutions, particularly any negative contact which could be problematic
- any social changes in the person's life, particularly changes in status (such as that associated with marriage breakdown, change of employment, migration, educational attainment); whether the person has lived through periods of social change, such as war, political upheaval or economic recession; how this has affected thinking, behaviour, life opportunities
- the person's attitude towards social and personal change; whether in possession of an ability to view social events broadly or see change as desirable or undesirable; whether able to cope with change

I am not suggesting that the radical caseworker must investigate all these aspects of every client's life—how much and what type of information is directly relevant depends on the specific situation and this principle applies to both traditionally or radically practised casework. However, what I am suggesting is that the caseworker needs to extend the traditional list of potential social information normally sought, to incorporate information about structural influences which might also be important.

A full list of both traditional and structural factors which may be important in assessing a person's situation is included in the Appendix.

SOCIAL EDUCATION

I have created the term 'social education' to refer to an education which focuses on both action and awareness. This differentiates it from training education which concentrates solely on skills

acquisition, or education which aims solely at increased understanding or insight. Social education in the action and awareness
sense is an idea common in feminist therapy and is broadly applicable to casework (Fook, 1986). It is similar to the concept of
'praxis', the combination of critical reflection on reality and subsequent action upon it described by Freire (1972:41) and referred
to under 'Developing critical awareness' in this chapter. The essence
of this type of educative process is that action and awareness must
always be coupled since neither can fully realise personal liberation
without the other. Concentrating solely on action can lead to the
manipulation of those being taught, whereas pure reflection can lead
to empty theorising (Freire, 1972:41). I have termed this educative
process 'social' simply because the main purpose of it, for the
radical caseworker, is to enable the individual person to act in the
social world. Although social education shares similar goals to those
of developing critical awareness, it includes a broader range of
techniques than those mainly verbal techniques normally associated
with conscientisation.

Educational techniques to foster this dual focus on action and
awareness would first include discussing potential actions with the
client every time a new awareness is reached; for example, parents
of a troublesome adolescent confiding that they may be a little too
strict, should be recognised and supported for this realisation, but
should also be presented with questions about what this will mean
for the parents in practical terms. Will they nag less? Will they allow
their teenager more responsibility? If so, how? What will they say
to her or him about this?

Secondly, each time activities are attempted or new skills learnt,
the person should be encouraged to reflect on what new awarenesses
have developed as a result. Using the above example, if the parents
try allowing the teenager sole responsibility for cleaning the bed-
room, the following questions could be discussed: in the parent's
opinion, has it worked or not? Why or why not? Do they have any
changed perceptions as a result? Do they feel any differently towards
their son or daughter? What did it feel like to allow more responsibility? Has it given any further ideas for action? The main aim in
examining these questions is not so much to find successful methods
for taming the teenager (although that is part of it). Rather it is to
help the parents critically reflect, so that they can make their own
links between what they think and what they do. This will in the
long term enable them to develop their personal resources to act
and exercise control in their social environment.

Caseworkers traditionally question clients about the reasons certain events occurred, or about clients' attitudes in order to collect
information which will help assess clients' situation. This can be

extended by the radical caseworker to encourage critical reflection, and awaken people to the possibilities of structural influences on their situation. The skill of critical questioning discussed earlier would be useful here. The skill of social empathy which will be discussed in detail further on, is also appropriate.

The gamut of behavioural modification techniques can be used to great advantage in a social educational strategy. For example, the technique of modelling may prove useful if the caseworker models the required behaviour, the client imitates it, and they both discuss their thoughts and feelings about the experience. Even techniques such as systematic desensitisation may be used in this context. With this technique, individuals' anxiety towards a certain object or situation is gradually reduced by their learning to cope with a list of increasingly anxiety-producing situations. For the purposes of education, client and worker need to discuss how the client's new-found ability to confront the previous impossible situation can have implications for other social aspects of life. For example, a person desensitised from a fear of spiders, can critically reflect upon not having this fear, and perhaps draw up a list of activities able to be attempted once the fear is conquered—for instance, to garden freely or go bushwalking.

ACTIVE USE OF RESOURCES

The 'active' use of resources refers to the types of strategies which encourage people to use resources in a way that furthers their control and autonomy. To encourage a person to actively use resources would involve using many of the techniques just discussed. An 'active' use of resources contrasts with a 'passive' use, where the user becomes dependent on an intermediate agent for access to the resources. For example, a pensioner is being encouraged to actively use resources if shown how to deal with counter staff directly, rather than passively requiring the repeated intervention of a social worker every time there is an interaction with front-line staff.

The caseworker can extend the passive use of resources to active use in various traditional areas described below.

Giving information

When giving information the client's autonomy can be maximised. The value of access to information in fostering equality in the casework relationship has already been noted. A similar principle holds in giving specific information about the client's environment (such as community resources). However, in this case, information is a resource for change rather than for negotiation, and for power equalisation with the worker.

In relation to this, it is important to make a distinction between two types of information: information which provides awareness, and information which enables action on that awareness; that is, there is a difference between providing information about something and information about how to use it. In keeping with the goal of social education and developing active use of resources, the radical caseworker should ensure that the client has both types of information. The name and telephone number of an agency, for example, is of minimal use to a person unless it's known why the agency may be of benefit and the procedure to follow for obtaining help there. In some cases (such as with people who have a developmental disability) imparting this type of knowledge may require the worker to actually transport the people to the agency and introduce them to the workers there. Although such an action seemingly contradicts social work dictums such as not encouraging dependency, a small degree of dependency in the initial stages may sometimes be necessary in order to impart the social knowledge and skills for ultimate autonomy. So practical information and actions are a necessary part of giving information and, like action and awareness in social education, they must be constantly linked.

To extend this point further, giving information to enable a person to actively use resources may require an element of giving skills to use the information. This type of approach may prove a useful adjunct to traditional psychologically based techniques, since many people who are helped by caseworkers often do not possess the requisite verbal or reflective capacities to fully benefit from solely therapeutic styles of help.

Referral

Similar principles may be applied in the processes of referring a client to use community resources. First, giving information about available community resources is obviously an essential part of a person's learning about the environment. Secondly, referral to other community resources is of minimal use unless the person is also informed of the reasons for the referral and is capable of following it up. Thirdly, a social education approach may also be applied. For example, the person may learn techniques for making enquiries of welfare services and being assertive in voicing their needs. These can be modelled after witnessing a competent referral with the caseworker, and a discussion of the whys and wherefores of the caseworker's behaviour.

Creative use of group and community resources

Individual autonomy can further be enhanced by fostering the person's ability to create alternative resources. In the last chapter we discussed how creating alternative support and status systems can combat oppression and exploitation in peoples' lives. The example quoted was that of families in which there was one member with a disability. Family members can often achieve personal satisfaction and social recognition through their work with voluntary groups. The same type of support and status can be developed with people who belong to other groups such as specific cultural or ethnic groups, leisure associations and so on. While advocating the joining or formation of groups for support of the client is a traditionally used strategy, seeing it as an extra source of status and power is less traditional. Thus, in a radical casework approach, social groups which may normally be socially devalued can become an alternative source of empowerment in the client's life.

Another potential alternative resource group for women clients in particular is other women in the community. Female clients can be encouraged to seek support and help from new and old acquaintances among women. In this way informal social networks of women may be utilised as a resource, and the female client can learn to renew old relationships for potential support. Where relevant, the client may be encouraged to formalise the network by organising regular meetings, or forming a recognised association or self-help group.

People who are significant in the client's life can be used in a similar way, as a substitute for regular contact with formal helping agencies. They may be people who can interact with, and potentially influence a person's life (Gambrill, 1983:215) and may be family members, friends, voluntary workers, or like-minded people with similar experiences.

Creative use of material resources

Material aid can also be given and used creatively, first by ensuring the client's autonomous access to and use of material aid, but also by creating alternative material resource systems. Encouraging clients to become members of, or to form co-operatives is a good example of this. Car pools and food co-ops are common examples of maximising the spread of benefits of material goods. Other possibilities might include lunch co-ops among low-income student groups.

As noted in the previous chapter, the rearrangement of resources in the physical environment can prove useful. On the large scale this may involve a process as ambitious as de-institutionalisation; for example, transferring bored and depressed psychiatric hospital inmates to a community setting to better learn social skills. On a smaller scale, furniture only might need moving and the decor improved and brightened in order to increase privacy or a sense of personal belonging (Gambrill, 1983:220).

SOCIAL EMPATHY

According to Carkhuff and Berenson (1979:9) empathy for a client involves the worker's 'ability to allow himself [sic] to experience or merge with the experience of the helpee, reflect upon this experience while suspending his [sic] own judgements, tolerating his [sic] own anxiety, and communicating this understanding to the helpee'. It is often assumed, from a definition such as this, that the experience to be reflected is confined to perceptions and feelings of the client's personal world. Unfortunately it is all too easy to overlook the client's perceptions, ideas and feelings about the social world. Accurate empathy should reflect all perceptions, ideas and feelings, since all are part of individual consciousness (Longres & McLeod, 1980:275). When beliefs about social situations or ideologies, are expressed, an empathic response ought to reflect these. This ability to empathise with the social content of the client's experience is here termed 'social empathy', and is a valuable tool for the radical caseworker to help link the personal and social in the client's situation.

Social empathy is also valuable for other reasons. First, empathic skills have much in common with skills to develop critical reflection (Keefe, 1980; Davies, 1983), and in communicating about shared experience, as discussed earlier. Secondly, when beliefs about social situations are expressed, an opportunity is presented to explore the client's social perceptions and how they impinge on life.

Take the following exclamation by a bored and depressed housewife: 'Men always get what they want!' This can be empathically reflected in at least two ways. The first picks up the personal experience: 'You feel you never get what you want?' The second highlights her perceptions of the social condition: 'You think men get a better deal than women?' A socially empathic response would ideally combine the two and draw attention to the links about them: 'You don't think you ever get what you want because men always get a better deal than women?'

The concept of social empathy is illustrated in more detail in an example from Egan (1982:89). He discusses the case of Peter, a student who has been 'exploring some developmental issues with one of the college counsellors'. Peter explains:

> I find biology really tough. I get through it, but I don't think I'm good enough to be in pre-med. I'm not going to make it into med school. It's not that I get distracted like some other guys—girls and drink and stuff like that. I frankly don't think I'm smart enough for pre-med. There's too much competition and it's not the only occupation in the world.

Let us begin to work out a socially empathic response by first analysing what Peter's concerns, both personal and social, might be. Among personal concerns hinted at are possible sexual ones (as Egan suggests in his discussion), but this also has a social component in that he couches this worry in terms of comparing himself to 'other guys'. He also has personal doubts about his intellectual ability to study biology, and links this with a belief about his social world; namely, that he is therefore 'not good enough to be in pre-med'. Indeed, it would appear that much of Peter's self-image and possibly esteem are related to his belief (and presumably what he thinks other people believe) about what personal capacities are necessary for success in a high status competitive occupation such as medicine. Therefore his personal worries about his sexuality and intellectual ability are related to social, career-choice types of concerns.

Having analysed possible personal and social concerns and the links between them, how then should we respond? An example of an empathic response which focuses mainly on Peter's personal concerns might be to say, 'You doubt that you've got what it takes to do medicine and you're starting to think you should do something else?' On the other hand, a socially empathic response which also picks up Peter's social beliefs and links them to his personal concerns might be to say, 'You're doubting your ability to do medicine because you think that those who succeed have to be smart and tough, and that, therefore, if you aren't succeeding you mustn't be smart or tough enough?'

This type of response focuses on how Peter's beliefs about his social world (in this case, his beliefs about the type of person who should be in medicine) may have coloured his beliefs about himself (not smart or tough) because he can't cut it in a smart, tough occupation. Provided Peter concurs with this analysis of his perceptions, the worker has created an opportunity to further explore the possible social origins of some of Peter's identity. In this way, Peter may be better able to make his career choice based on his personal preferences, rather than on what he thinks are the social expectations of those who achieve in a high status profession. The worker could thus follow the initial socially empathic response by asking the following: 'If you think you can't cut it for these reasons, I wonder whether your decision to change courses might be based on what you think are the social expectations of people who succeed at medicine, rather than on what you personally want to do?' Discussion about how 'true' these expectations are, and what Peter's personal wishes and abilities are, unclouded by social expectations, could then follow. In this way, social empathy can be used as a technique to develop critical awareness and to create clearer choices and alternatives for people. An exercise on social empathy is included in the Appendix.

SOCIAL SUPPORT

Supportive or sustaining techniques traditionally used in casework cover a range of skills designed to communicate acceptance, calm anxiety and generally assure and encourage the client (Hollis, 1964:83–8). Again, as with empathy, it is all too easy to confine supportive skills to bolstering the psychological well-being of the client. Although this of course is vital, clients may also need support to help them master situations caused by the social aspect of their lives. For this reason, the term 'social support' is used here to emphasise techniques which also support clients' efforts to act in their social environments. This is not to deny that people do not experience emotional difficulties. Where this is the case, the worker must also supply emotional support. However, it is not always enough for the radical caseworker to confine reassurance to lessening emotional trauma.

There are a number of ways in which a radical caseworker can extend traditional sustaining techniques to support the client in social endeavours, and in the personal change often required when assuming control in one's life. First, as has been discussed in an earlier section, developing alternative support or status networks can help clients cope with any new social behaviour they may exhibit. For example, a mature-age woman who takes up formal study may encounter some derision from uneducated friends or family. She will derive social support by cultivating alternative friendships with like-minded women who value what she is doing.

Secondly, the provision of positive social experiences can give a person a more acceptable personal social identity. Wolfensberger's concept of 'social role valorisation' (1983) illustrates this nicely. This refers to the idea that the best way to 'normalise' people who belong to socially devalued groups is to create, support and defend valued social roles for them (Steer, 19089:43). Typically this might involve, for example, ensuring that people with disabilities have meaningful, important work which would otherwise have to be done by someone else, rather than boring, repetitious work which is created simply to occupy them.

Thirdly, a large part of the social support provided by radical caseworkers may involve supporting the person in taking risks, coping with change, and trying out new roles and behaviours. The person may need to be prepared for change, and reassured that it may take a long and painful time, but that it is also possible and rewarding. The caseworker may need to accompany the client on the first of new ventures, or may need to 'pick up the pieces' each time something new is tried.

Social support may also take the form of supporting people when they encounter any social or interpersonal resistance to the changes they have chosen to make. This may involve withstanding any derogatory interpretations of their new behaviour. They may have to deal with conflict, aggression, physical violence, misunderstanding or emotional blackmail. Take, for example, the sequence of problems that may confront a young mother whose son is assessed as having a behaviour problem. She may also aim to have some regular release from child care in order to undertake a course of study. Women friends may accuse her of being unrealistic; however, the caseworker should help her affirm her choice as feasible. Her husband may be openly hostile when initially faced with the request to take more responsibility with their son. The worker may help the woman see this anger as a predictable reaction to change, and support her position until the resistance is resolved. If her husband's hostility does not abate, the woman may need help to re-evaluate her choices in the light of this new situation by putting up with her husband's anger or giving way on her choice; or she may need help to deal with this anger. Her own mother may strongly disapprove and interpret this behaviour as evidence of her own failure to raise her daughter properly. The client may then need support in reaffirming her decision, and resisting any tendency to feel responsible for her mother's expectations. In pursuing her studies the client might find that classes are timetabled at late and irregular hours, making it difficult to plan child care arrangements with her husband. The worker may need to support her in seeking alternative timetabling arrangements with the educational institution, or in making child care plans with her husband or child care agency.

EVALUATION OF CASEWORK OUTCOME

Evaluation is crucial to radical casework. The ability to reflect and act upon one's social world is an integral part of developing critical awareness and should be done by both client and worker together in an ongoing way simply through the continual dual focus on action and awareness. However, a checklist of questions derived from the original assessment and goals of radical casework may also be useful in helping worker and client decide whether the goals have been achieved when coming towards the end of the professional contact. Specific items for evaluation will depend on the specific goals the worker and client initially agreed upon; however, Sturdivant (1980:173) lists some items which feminist therapists use to assess their work with a female client. These may also be applicable in radical casework:

- What is the connection between the pain, the symptoms and the life situation?
- Are there any growing pains?
- Is their self-esteem dependent on others?
- Are their ideals and role choices based on traditional stereotypes?
- Does their interpersonal style allow for a full range of behaviour?
- Can they relate to both sexes as people? Can they draw support from other women?
- Is their role pattern their own choice?
- Do they trust in their own decision making?

To these might be added:

- Can they accept and cope with change?
- Have they received the full range of social service benefits to which they are entitled?
- Are they fully aware of the community resources for future need?
- Do they know how to use them?
- Do they have potential support systems?

8   Cases

This chapter details six cases to illustrate how radical casework might be conducted based on the guidelines we have established. Some of the cases are taken from real situations changed to obscure the identities of parties involved; others are composite cases constructed from a number of situations. After describing each case I have outlined a case plan comprising an assessment of the problem and causes, casework goals and suggestions for practice strategies. Each case plan uses a radical framework incorporating some traditional elements but extending them to a structural breadth in order to illustrate in some detail how a radical approach might hypothetically work in a specific situation. Following each radical case plan is a plan using non-radical approaches, thereby illustrating the differences of the radical approach.

Naturally I am not arguing that each presentation represents the *only* way to approach the particular case, from either a radical or non-radical perspective. The case plans included here are intended only as hypothetical illustrations outlining the different directions and scope of the radical and non-radical frameworks.

CASE 1   HELEN KELP

Helen Kelp is a 24-year-old woman with a borderline intellectual disability (IQ tested at around 70). She also suffers from epilepsy. She lives with her parents (John and Marion Kelp, in their mid-forties) and younger brother Stephen (14) in a lower middle class

area of a small industrial city. Helen's sister, Liz (26), is married
and has a young baby. She lives nearby.

Helen works in sheltered employment in a workshop run by a
local voluntary community-based agency. She is referred to the
social worker who works for the voluntary organisation because she
is classed as a 'behaviour problem' by the workshop staff. They
complain that she is disobedient, hides things, and keeps getting up
from the work table.

The social worker interviews Helen at the workshop. She is neatly
dressed, attractive and quietly spoken. She is eager to talk to the
worker and quite articulate. Although she agrees with the complaints
of the workshop staff about her behaviour, she says she does not
know why she does these things. She prefers to talk about other
issues—that she is unhappy at home, and feels she is treated like a
child and not given any responsibility. She feels she is forced to go
to church and is not allowed out alone. Her parents punish her
disobedience at home by not allowing her to attend social outings
organised by various voluntary associations for people with disabilities. Helen does not have any friends her own age outside the
workshop situation. She gets on with her brother Stephen, although
she feels jealous that he is allowed more responsibility. She spends
some time at her sister Liz's place, and enjoys helping her look
after the baby.

The social worker then interviews John, Marion and Helen at
home regarding Helen's problems at the workshop. Both John and
Marion consider Helen to be a problem in general. She is 'disobedient', 'cheeky', 'immature' and 'irresponsible'. They do not believe
that she will ever be able to leave home or be independent. They
feel somewhat resentful of this, as they do not like to picture
themselves looking after Helen for the rest of their lives. They are
also anxious about her welfare. Marion Kelp reports that Helen has
in fact 'run away' from home several times; that is, she has left the
house for a day and not told anyone that she is going or where she
is going. Her parents have become frantic at these times.

Both Helen and her parents seem less concerned about Helen's
behaviour in the workshop than about her general situation. They
all ask whether the social worker can do something about the
situation.

Case Plans

Radical approach

1 Assessment There are two main, inter-related problems here: the
problem of Helen's behaviour at work (the original referral), and the

problem in general of Helen's present and future living arrangements (raised by Helen and her parents).

It would seem that, for the most part, Helen's behaviour is defined as problematic by a number of parties, two of whom are in positions of power over Helen (workshop staff and her parents). Workshop staff believe she is disruptive in the workplace. Her parents believe her behaviour disrupts their present and future lives. Helen herself is more concerned about the behaviour of her parents in disallowing her freedom.

A major question which needs to be answered in addressing the problem is whose interests are being served by the referral? The original referral was made in the interests of workshop management, but on investigation there are a number of other interests which can also be served—those of both Helen and her parents. In this case interests do not necessarily compete, but are not necessarily congruent either. For example, the workshop staff may only be satisfied if Helen conforms to workshop rules, and Helen's parents may wish her to behave more responsibly so that she can become independent; Helen herself may simply wish for more freedom and to be treated like an adult. Before deciding what action to take, the radical caseworker will need to determine whether all interests can be served satisfactorily, or whether some may need to take precedence over others.

A major part of the problem may be how 'problems' are defined by all the participants and the stereotyped expectations which underlie them. Helen has been defined as a problem because her behaviour is deviant and disrupts the running of the workplace and the home. She is not satisfactorily performing the roles of dutiful worker or daughter. She is also caught in role conflict: on the one hand it is expected that she act like a responsible adult, but on the other she is treated like a naughty and recalcitrant child with a disability. In terms of social expectations, the role of a 'person with a disability' is not a fully adult independent one. We see this clearly played out in Helen's case, and we see the influence of social labelling as well—the tendency to 'label' Helen as having an intellectual disability, placing her in sheltered employment with other workers performing below her capacity, and (on her parents' part) redefining any non-conformity as 'childish' rather than an act of individuality. Her behaviour, though annoying, is understandable if it is seen as an attempt of a relatively powerless person to gain some power. She uses the only avenues at her disposal—to disrupt normal routine—rather than attempt to reason or argue her points for which first, she probably lacks the intellectual capacity, and secondly, she would probably not be taken seriously if she did try to.

Helen's parents too are caught up in social expectations regarding people with intellectual disabilities. They assume that their role must always be that of guardian and caretaker, believing along with most people that Helen is incapable of becoming independent. Their views of her have changed little since she was a child, when there was a marked lack of resources to assist people like Helen towards independent living. They are not necessarily parents who are denying their child's ability and refusing to let her go and become independent. Rather, they may not have caught up with changing times, and the fact that there are now services which can assist Helen towards independence (community housing, social skills programs, respite care). Helen's parents have become used to having to manage on their own, and are doing so to the best of their ability. They are not 'bad' parents if they need to rely on the resources provided by other people to help Helen towards independence.

The concerns of Helen's parents may also be very realistic given current social conditions of violence and sexual crimes against women. Coupled with their religious background they may be understandably concerned about Helen's sexual safety at the times she goes 'missing'.

Likewise, workshop staff may be working in a system which only encourages maximum 'process line' output from workers, and does not reward individual or creative effort. They do not have the time to attend to Helen's personal work needs and become seriously concerned about the survival of the workshop if behaviour like Helen's is too disruptive.

In summary then, Helen's disruptive behaviour may be seen as an act on her part to gain some power in a situation where she is virtually powerless. This behaviour in turn is defined as 'problematic' or deviant because it does not conform to the interests of the more powerful groups in Helen's life (workshop staff and parents). Helen is caught in a contradiction: she is labelled as 'disabled' and, therefore, 'childish and dependent' yet still expected to act 'adult', 'responsible' and, by implication, 'independent'. She is treated as dependent yet expected to behave independently.

2 Casework goals Given the above assessment, is it possible to meet the interests of all groups involved or are some necessarily competing? In this case I think it is possible, by empowering Helen and, thereby, increasing her ability to act responsibly and more like an adult, that all interest groups may be satisfied. If Helen does, in fact, act more responsibly she will be less of a problem at home and in the workshop and may achieve her own goals of independence. The main aim, therefore, will be to give Helen more power. This will involve changing stereotyped views of Helen on the part of workshop staff and her parents, and increasing awareness of the social-labelling process on

the part of everyone. Material restrictions (lack of services) which
contribute to Helen's dependence need also to be addressed.

3 Suggested strategies
   a Bureaucratic techniques. Show how workshop requirements
      can dampen the creative abilities of some workers. Provide
      social work assessment of Helen's abilities to workshop staff.
      Assume the role of advocate for Helen with workshop staff.
      Help devise a work program which will better use her abilities
      in activities which are less routine and more creative. See
      whether there are some existing activities performed by work-
      shop staff that Helen could assist with which would give her
      more actual responsibility.
   b Empowerment techniques. Give Helen some powerful experi-
      ences away from her parents. For example, see whether she
      can be of some real assistance to her sister Liz with the baby
      and see whether there are some activities she can be solely
      responsible for herself. Draw up a list of things she already
      does successfully at home, and devise some others to work
      towards. Ensure that Helen is allowed to do these on her own,
      exercising her own choice about how they are to be done.
   c Develop critical awareness. Help Helen's parents see how
      their views of Helen may be contradictory, partly based on
      social expectations about people with disabilities, but also
      based on outdated assumptions about resources for people
      with disabilities. Help Helen to see how she has been
      'labelled', and how her own behaviour contributes to that
      labelling. Help them all create alternative roles for Helen
      within the family, not just as wholly independent or depend-
      ent, but as independent with some things and dependent with
      others. For example, she can go independently to Liz's to help
      with the baby, and choose which activities she can help with,
      but she cannot necessarily be independent enough to look after
      the baby for a whole day on her own.
   d Creative use of resources. Encourage the Kelps to use other
      services which might help Helen become independent (for
      example, supervised holiday trips, staying with relatives).
      Give the family as much information as possible about the
      available services and discuss the pros and cons of using one
      critically so that they all (Helen included) make an informed
      choice about them. If they dislike using government services,
      encourage them to use others creatively. For example, they
      might prefer Helen to slot in with more of the church activ-
      ities. Encourage them to do this if Helen can be allowed more
      responsibility in choosing which ones she joins.

Non-radical approach

1 Assessment The problem of Helen's workshop behaviour may simply be treated as a behaviour problem which is triggered by particular stimuli. Perhaps workshop staff are paying her more negative attention than other workers and 'picking on' her. Perhaps other workers are teasing her or daring her to misbehave. Similar processes may be happening at home. There may be a sense of rivalry with Helen's younger brother Stephen, and she may be jealous of his relative freedom; therefore, every time he taunts her she misbehaves accordingly.

Alternatively, the problem at home may be viewed as one of family communication, resulting from some of the difficulties her parents have in coming to terms with Helen as a person. Helen misbehaves because she is being given conflicting messages that she is expected to be an 'adult' yet is being treated as a 'child'. These mixed messages given by her parents may be the result of their inability to cope with Helen's transition to adulthood. They may also feel some ambivalence because their care is not sufficient for her needs, but they feel guilty that they cannot give unconditional care and regard. They are possibly also simply being over-protective—unable to cope with the idea that Helen is growing up and has rights of her own. Given their religious views they may also be over-anxious about Helen's sexual awareness and involvement, and unable to cope with the idea that she can be a sexual being. Hence, their anxiety on the days she goes 'missing'.

2 Casework goals Based on these views of the problem, the goals may be to modify Helen's behaviour at work and home, and to improve family communication.

3 Strategies
  a A behaviour modification program might need to be worked out for Helen both at work and home. She might be induced to respond in different, more positive ways when she is taunted by other workers or her brother.
  b Personal counselling for Helen might help her to see how her behaviour is disruptive for other people, and motivate her to change it.
  c Family counselling or therapy might address the problem of family communication. All family members can be shown how their attitudes towards Helen and beliefs about her capabilities affect her behaviour, and may learn to work together as a family unit in assisting Helen towards independence.
  d Personal counselling for either John, Marion or both regarding their feelings of ambivalence and guilt about Helen's care may

resolve their contradictory fears and anxieties about her future. This could include giving them concrete information about Helen's capabilities. Personal counselling could also address their feelings about Helen's sexuality and help them cope with this.

CASE 2 TONY KELLY

Eighteen-year-old Tony Kelly lives in a large private hostel run by a family (employing some qualified psychiatric nurses) as a profit-making concern. It houses mainly young single people, many with mild disabilities. Tony is part-Aboriginal and has mild brain damage as a result of a car accident several years earlier. He is referred to a social worker at a local community health centre by the hostel manager because of problems he is causing at the hostel. He refuses to clean his room, argues with the residents, often comes home drunk and damages his room and the general living area. He is suspected of sexual promiscuity, particularly with female residents in the hostel, and it is also rumoured among residents (although there are no definite claims) that he had attempted to sexually assault two women who have since left the hostel. He has lived at the hostel for five months, and for the first four months there were no problems. He will not discuss the reasons for his more recent behaviour with the manager, and has not responded to requests to co-operate with hostel rules. The manager is reluctant to evict him without some further attempt to address his problems.

An interview between Tony and the worker is arranged by the manager at the hostel. Tony is unwilling to see the worker but has been told by the manager that unless he does, he will have to leave the hostel immediately. At first he is surly and hostile towards the worker but softens when he realises the worker is prepared to hear his side of the story. He admits that he has caused some damage but he believes that the hostel residents are ganging up on him and spreading rumours about him because he is an Aborigine. He has no friends at the hostel. He has no family with whom he can live. His mother threw him out of home five months before because he had an argument with her new boyfriend, and his younger brother now lives on the streets. Tony works in sheltered employment and through staff there gained accommodation in the present hostel. He has one friend, a girl he met through work (Helen Kelp, see case 1) a couple of months ago, with whom he gets on quite well. Helen's parents do not approve of their friendship. Helen has been 'sneaking out' to see him some days on weekends, but her parents have now threatened to take her away from work if she continues to see him.

Tony is very angry and hurt about all this and cannot understand
'what they have against me'. He does not know what he will do if
he has to leave the hostel, but continually tells the worker 'I can
handle myself'. He wouldn't mind staying at the hostel if 'they all
leave me alone and get off my back', but he would not mind going
somewhere else either. He agrees his behaviour has not been good,
but blames the manager and residents for setting him off. He would
really like the worker to 'get them all off my back'.

Case plans

Radical approach

1 Assessment The main presenting problem for Tony is to find some
accommodation or to change his behaviour so that he can remain where
he is at present. Although Tony has undoubtedly been 'wronged
against', it would also appear that he has done some 'wronging' against
others in the hostel. The difficult issue in this case will be to handle all
competing interests fairly. The fact that Tony seems reluctant to accept
any blame for the present situation complicates matters. In this sense
he is an involuntary client.

There are many possible social reasons for Tony's present situation. He definitely comes from a disadvantaged background, without
support from family, or his own financial resources to fall back on.
He has experienced, and is experiencing, a great deal of social
rejection: from his mother in the past, hostel residents, and now
Helen's parents. His disability means he has little prospect of full
financial and social independence, so his behaviour will always be
of concern to others, since it is likely that he will always have to
live in shared accommodation of some kind. The possibility that he
will be labelled a 'problem' is, therefore, greater for Tony than an
average member of the population. He may indeed be subjected to
some racism (and labelling) in the hostel, which could (at least
partly) account for some of the rumours about his sexual activity,
and may account for his anger and subsequent behaviour towards
hostel residents. The fact that he will not accept any personal
responsibility for the situation is not a socially attractive attitude on
his part, but may be a racial adaptation he has had to make. It may
be a defensive position he has had to learn to take from prior
dealings with white Australians who have sought to blame him
wrongfully. It may also simply indicate his lack of trust of the
worker, both personally and as a representative of the white Australian exploitative structure. In the same way, anger and physical
violence may be the main socially acceptable ways he has learnt to
react to social rejection.

Despite the reasonable social explanations for Tony's behaviour, this does not excuse it and mean it can be ignored or condoned. The social reality is that Tony must coexist with other people. Other people in his environs have a right not to be harmed by his behaviour. If all the claims about him are true, some of his behaviour is illegal and, at the very least, offensive, no matter what the reasons are for it. Other people (hostel manager and residents) have a right to ask that this behaviour cease, and a right to ask to leave if he does not abide by the regulations of the hostel.

What needs to be discerned here is how much of the situation is actually caused by the hostel, and how much by Tony, so that relative interests can be juggled to suit all parties. Even if Tony leaves this hostel, he will still need to change his behaviour, because it is unlikely it would be tolerated anywhere else. And if Tony leaves the hostel, the manager and residents will still need to examine and possibly change their practices to ensure that a similar situation does not occur with anyone else. Without further information, it seems reasonable to posit at this point that Tony's anger might be provoked by other people (for example, racist hostel residents, Helen's disapproving parents), but that the way he chooses to vent his anger (physical violence and the consequences of this) is his responsibility.

2 Casework goals The main, ultimate goal in this case is to resolve Tony's accommodation problem. This might, however, involve having to modify some of his and the hostel's practices, specifically Tony's violent behaviour (including sexual violence), and the hostel's racism.

3 Suggested strategies
   a Bureaucratic techniques. Assume the role of advocate on Tony's behalf with hostel management. Work with hostel manager to examine hostel situation and the possible racist behaviour of residents (and management as well). This may involve developing some critical awareness; for example, making them aware of how and when they label Tony, and how it makes him feel and behave. It also may involve challenging any 'myths' or prejudices they may hold about him or Aboriginal people. Devise program to censure this behaviour within the hostel.
   b Develop critical awareness. Show how the labelling attitudes of hostel residents cause him to behave in that way, but that he really has a choice about how he reacts. Empower him by making clearer his choices of responses (for example, a smart retort, ignoring them, going into his room and shutting the door).
   c Empowerment technique. Give some powerful experiences by concentrating on his positive attributes and ask hostel manager

to help with this. For example, find out what Tony is good at
or interested in and see whether he can be made responsible
for it at the hostel. Show him the power he already has in the
situation, such as having choices about whether he goes or
stays, how he reacts to hostel residents, whether he stays in
his room or not, and so on. Make him aware that he is making
choices about each of these, and what is involved in each of
the choices. Show how other people also make choices, and
how his choices also influence theirs.

d Equalise power imbalances. Get Tony and the hostel manager
and residents to work together on agreements about generally
acceptable behaviour, including violent behaviour, but also
any racist behaviour, scapegoating or labelling. Clarify what
behaviour is acceptable and what is not in which circumstances, and what the consequences are. For example, any
claims of sexual assault must be reported directly to the hostel
manager, who may call the police. Any overheard racist com-
ments (which must be defined) must be reported.

Non-radical approach

1 Assessment The main problem is to curb and modify Tony's deviant
and unacceptable behaviour. His behaviour would be a problem in any
situation in which he was to live, therefore it is necessary to work on
it so that he can become a more acceptable resident.

Tony exhibits a number of personality traits which are disturbing:
a lack of insight; a tendency to blame or project on to others; an
immature inability to accept responsibility for his own actions. He
is still very much the egocentric adolescent with his inability to
understand other viewpoints, his false bravado and his 'paranoia'
towards hostel residents. His limited intellectual abilities as a result
of his brain damage probably mean that he has limited ability to
find other accommodation, therefore it is important that he learn to
conform to the requirements of the present hostel.

He seems to be a particularly socially isolated young man, therefore it is more difficult for him to learn normal social skills. This
would be exacerbated by his background, and obviously non-sup-
portive relationship with his mother. There may also be communication problems between the hostel manager and Tony, since Tony
seems to be able to talk satisfactorily to the social worker. This may
also be the case between him and other hostel residents. Perhaps
they misunderstand him, and have scapegoated him as the deviant
member of the hostel.

In summary, his social isolation coupled with his own personal and intellectual limitations probably indicate that some form of behaviour modification is most appropriate.

2 Casework goals Modify Tony's behaviour so that he is able to express his anger in non-violent ways, and discourage sexual promiscuity (and the possibility of him committing any sexual assaults).

3 Suggested strategies
   a   Behaviour modification. Construct a behavioural regime for Tony and work on selected behaviours separately. Hostel manager, residents and even staff at his workplace may be enlisted to help.
   b   Counselling, modelling and role playing. Discuss alternative ways of expressing anger, and model and role play these with Tony.
   c   Refer to a social skills group. Some of the above might be covered in this group.

CASE 3   CON DRAKOPOULOS

Con Drakopoulos (35) is referred to the social worker in the Department of Social Security. For two years Con has been receiving a benefit for temporary illness incapacitating him for regular work, and is referred to the social worker by one of the clerical officers for assessment regarding his eligibility to continue in receipt of this benefit.

The social worker visits Con and his wife Maria (30) and their two daughters (two and four years old) at their small home in an inner-city area of a large metropolitan city. The area is crowded and noisy, with few recreational facilities, and is one of the as yet 'ungentrified' inner areas of the city. Con ceased full-time work as a builder's labourer two years ago when he began to suffer from an increasing number of back pains, and dizzy and nausea spells. Since then he has tried various part-time jobs in a takeaway (fish and chips) food shop owned by friends, but was unable to continue because of nausea and severe headaches.

Con mostly spends his time at home sleeping or watching TV. He tries reading but it brings on headaches. He says he is often bored, but also enjoys doing very little. He is quietly spoken and expresses little strong emotion. One of his few social contacts is a Greek psychologist whom Con has been seeing fortnightly for the last six months, and who charges $80 per session. Con says he likes talking to him as he cannot talk to his friends about his problems, but he doesn't feel he is being helped with his illnesses.

Con migrated to Australia from a rural village in Greece eleven years previously. Maria joined him six years ago to be married. They had become engaged in Greece and planned that Con should migrate first to set up a home for Maria. It took Con five years to save enough for Maria's fare and a deposit on a house. About four years ago Con took on two jobs as they were not able to meet house-mortgage loan repayments. Con worked eighteen hours a day, and usually weekends.

Con says his main worries are to provide an education for his children and a home for Maria. He is vague about current finances and says they are managing all right. During the interview Maria has hovered in the background, but she sees the social worker to the door and pleads that something be done for Con as she is very worried about him.

Case Plans

Radical approach

1 Assessment The main problems in this case are that of Con's illness and financial security for the Drakopoulos family. Their financial security is threatened, both for social and bureaucratic reasons. Con is unable to work to support the family, and it is likely that for cultural and other social reasons, he sees this as his role, not his wife's. Also, his eligibility for continuing government support is threatened as his case undergoes a review.

Con's illness is understandable in the light of his background; the expectations he would have had as a migrant wishing to succeed in his adopted country have placed heavy pressures on him emotionally, socially and financially. He takes his social role as a father, husband and breadwinner very seriously, as well as his role as a new migrant trying to make good. There are very real social and material restrictions on him which make it difficult for him to succeed in these roles: the barriers of language; the hard physical labour involved in most of the jobs which are available to him; the over-work involved in holding down two jobs at once; the difficulties of social and emotional adjustment, both between countries and between rural and urban life; and the years of social and emotional isolation as he toiled to prepare a home for his bride. There may also be cultural reasons for the type of illness he suffers from, and his attitude towards it. He may feel shamed by his inability to provide adequately for his family, and his illness may provide a socially acceptable reason for not being able to work.

Con's social isolation may in part be his choice, as he may feel ashamed by his position and, therefore, reluctant to mix with friends or discuss it openly. Since he comes from a rural background, he may believe the psychologist is an important person or patron (see Huber, 1984) who should be able to help him and, therefore, will continue to see him whether he is helped or not.

Con is very much a man caught up in a extremely difficult social situation which has been placing extraordinary demands on him. As a migrant, his personal and social and family expectations to succeed are added to the pressures of having to adjust to a quite different country, culture and urban environment as well. He is without the normal supports on which he would draw, in an environment which is relatively unfamiliar on most counts.

2 Casework goals The main aim in this case is to try to ensure some financial security for the Drakopoulos family as well as link Con with some resources to relieve his illness.

3 Suggested strategies
  a Bureaucratic techniques. Investigate the possibility of other pensions or benefits which might be more appropriate for Con. Find out how much flexibility or discretion is involved in eligibility for his current benefit. Arrange for Con to receive the payments which will benefit him the most.
  b Creative use of resources. Link Con up with a social worker, psychologist or psychiatrist who may understand his particular cultural approach to his problem and help him face it. This may be appropriate with the psychologist Con is already seeing. The worker would need to make sure that this psychologist was not simply exploiting his relationship with Con as a fellow Greek. See what other resources already exist within the Greek community that Con would not feel ashamed to use. It may be that Con would feel less shamed to mix outside his immediate community, with people he does not already know. It may also be worth investigating other sources of finance. If Con says they are managing all right, is this because he does not wish to acknowledge his plight to the worker, or are there in fact other sources of help on which he is relying (for example, friends)?
  c Develop critical awareness. In empathising with Con's situation, help him see how it is similar to the social situation of many migrants. Try to reduce any self-blame by presenting to him the difficulties which he has already overcome, and perhaps try to set more realistic or manageable expectations. This should help to reduce pressure and stress on him.
  d Provide social support for Maria. Encourage Maria to seek the company and support of other Greek women.

Non-radical approach

1 Assessment The main problem is Con's inability to provide for his family, and the possibility that he may no longer be eligible to continue receiving his present benefits. It seems he has been unable to cope with the stress of his previous work, and is deteriorating both physically and emotionally as a result. There seems to be little prospect of improvement in the current situation unless moves are made to seek further or different assistant from that which he has received to date. He seems little motivated to do this. In fact, his wife is the only person who actually requests help. Con may be becoming gradually more depressed so that he sees little hope of getting better and returning to work. He does not seem to have recently consulted with a medical practitioner about his illness, so it is possible that he is simply assuming nothing can be done. There does seem to be some acceptance that the problem may be an emotional one, hence the regular consultation with the psychologist. Given his cultural background, this might be a difficult admission to make.

There is the possibility of financial mismanagement considering the Drakopoulos' financially straitened circumstances, Con's vagueness about exact financial details, and his regular payment of $80 per session to the psychologist. The situation seems one of little hope unless something can change the current system. A continuation of current benefits might only perpetuate the hopeless situation.

2 Casework goals The main aim would be to try and introduce some change into the system in order to motivate some change on Con's part, to hopefully aid his return to work.

3 Suggested strategies
 a   Try to get Maria to go to work and take over the breadwinning role. This might shame Con into trying to work again, by seeing that his role is being usurped. Build on Maria's strengths to keep the family functioning.
 b   Recommend the cessation of current benefits, or a continuation of current benefits on the proviso that there is much more regular monitoring, and that Con seek further assistance for stress management.
 c   Arrange for Con to have another full medical assessment to determine the current nature of his illness and possible causes.
 d   Assess the family's financial situation and arrange for financial counselling if necessary.

CASE 4   FRANCES TURNER

Frances Turner (38) seeks the assistance of her local community-

health social worker in a small rural town, on the recommendation
of her church minister. She has been reluctant to seek professional
help, and has only done so out of desperation. Frances says she has
a marriage problem, and has been apprehensive about seeking professional help as her husband George (47) is training to be psychiatrist, and she knows many of the local professionals personally and
feels too embarrassed to approach them. She asks whether she can
see the worker on a private basis so that townspeople will not
suspect that she is receiving professional help. The worker agrees
to visit her once at home to see what the problem is and whether
she can offer Frances any help.

Frances says her problem is that neither George nor her sons
(Garth, 17 and Darren, 12) actually care about her. She feels alone
and untrusted by George, who will not discuss his work with her
because she 'wouldn't understand'. She feels she is uninteresting
and unintelligent. She agrees with her mother-in-law Sophia (65),
who raised George as a single mother and worked long hours as a
housekeeper to support him through his medical study, that her main
duty is to make a home for George and the boys, but she feels she
is failing at this. Sometimes she regrets her past life, wishing she
had never married and had children, but wonders whether she would
have had the ability to pursue a career anyway. Her parents had
wanted her to become a doctor (her father is prominent in the
medical profession in a large neighbouring city). Frances' doubts
and confusion have been building up for some time, but she now
feels she desperately needs to do something as Sophia has decided
she wants to come and live with George and Frances because she
has arthritis and needs assistance with day-to-day housework.
George seems fairly indifferent to this, but Frances is fearful that
if she refuses Sophia's request (which she is very unhappy about),
it will be the end of the marriage. She also feels that if Sophia does
come to stay it will be the end of any happiness she might have
now.

Frances and George met while both studying medicine nineteen
years ago. They lived together briefly and married before Garth was
born. Frances ceased her study at this time, then tried to resume
medical studies shortly afterwards but found it 'too demanding'.
Over the years since, she has tried (unsuccessfully) to complete
several other courses (psychology, an arts degree, and certificate in
welfare work). She decided to have her younger son Darren after
continued pressure from George and Sophia. She also felt that
'maybe mothering was the only thing I could do well'. George and
Frances moved to the country town where they now live five years
ago to be closer to Sophia. Frances has considered study towards a

social work degree, but there is no local university which offers the course.

Case Plans

Radical approach

1 Assessment The presenting problem is two-fold: Frances' belief that she has a marriage problem, and the potential conflict looming in the mother-in-law Sophia wanting to come to live.

Frances' belief that she has a marriage problem appears based on her conviction that she is unloved (by her sons as well as husband), and that she probably deserves their indifference because she is unworthy of their esteem. She has a marked lack of regard for her own abilities. Much of this seems to be caused by her confusion and probable guilt about the appropriate social role for her as a woman, wife and mother. The fact that she defines her problem as a marriage problem indicates her beliefs about the importance of marriage, which may be socially influenced. She is very much a woman caught up in the changing trends towards women's achievements outside the home, and her mother-in-law's objections to this and, therefore, conflict regarding this in the home.

She herself has some fairly traditional views about her expected role as a wife, mother and daughter-in-law, and experiences some conflict in her own mind about this. This conflict is exacerbated by a number of external factors including George's profession as a medical practitioner and trainee psychiatrist which probably means that, in line with the traditional conservatism of this established profession, he is unsympathetic to any of her needs or wishes for a career. It is also most unlikely, given the demands of his profession, that he would spend much energy attending to the needs of his family. He would need and expect Frances to do this. As well, George's (and Sophia's) own social background means that he probably expects a woman to subjugate her needs to those of her husband and to other domestic duties. Sophia subjugated her own needs to provide for George's future—a not uncommon story for many single mothers of that generation. This reflects the restricted social roles and avenues for personal satisfaction available to women in past times. Her only opportunity to achieve social standing is through her son's achievements, and she would expect Frances to support him (and her) in this. She would probably believe that her own care would be part of France's duty to George as her husband. Frances seems to believe this as well, as evidenced by her fear that if she refuses Sophia's request, it will be the end of the marriage.

There are, too, conflicts for Frances caused by contrasting her

own upbringing to that of George, and her own present circumstances. There is a class difference between Frances' and George's
background, which may in part cause them to hold different ideologies about the importance of career and education (especially for
women).

A further problem is that of adequate resources in relation to
Sophia; that is, a shortage of appropriate services to enable elderly
people to remain independently in their own homes. This reflects a
structural shortcoming and the present-day tendency to live in a
nuclear family unit which is economically and socially independent.

Because they live in a rural area, Frances is unable to undertake
the type of study she wishes. This is part of a two-fold structural
problem: that of rural disadvantage, and that of the problem of the
inaccessibility of study opportunities for women. Frances is disadvantaged on both counts.

In summary, Frances seems depressed as a result of her confusion
and conflict (with other family members) about appropriate social
roles for herself as a woman. She blames herself and the marriage
for this confusion and conflict, rather than seeing them as brought
about by current social trends, and by conflicts over position with
more powerful members of the family (George and Sophia). She
seems to have learnt to blame herself (failure to complete courses
of study has been defined as some inadequacy in herself rather than
as caused by an impediment in her situation; for example, the birth
of Garth), partly through explicit pressure (and possible exploitation) from family members.

2 Casework goals The main aims are to empower Frances by reducing
her self-blame (and, therefore, depression); to help clarify and/or
resolve some of the conflict regarding her social role; to decrease
George and Sophia's apparent exploitation of her; and to clarify and
discover some care options for Sophia.

3 Suggested strategies
   a   Critical questioning. This may assist Frances to clarify her
       own views and separate them from the pressures and expec-
       tations of others (whether it be of George and Sophia or
       general social expectations). This may also help reduce her
       self-blame: she may be able to see more clearly which aspects
       of her problem she is responsible for, and which are caused
       by others.
   b   Creating alternatives. Techniques to create some other ways
       to meet Sophia's care needs may help Frances' situation. For
       example, Sophia living with Frances and George may not be
       the only option. Help Frances (and/or Sophia and George if

they wish to be involved) to creatively imagine options regarding living arrangements, and then examine what is practically possible.

c   Advocacy. The worker may act as an advocate for Frances within the family situation if she does not feel capable of expressing her own wishes to them.

d   Empowerment techniques. Giving Frances some powerful experiences like performing voluntary work, or involvement in community work can help to reduce self-blame.

e   Creating alternative social support and status networks. This could also help empower Frances, but also provide additional emotional and social support. She could be encouraged to revive stronger links with her family of origin, or she could be encouraged to start her own group in her local community around some interest she already has (for example, a book club, discussion group, women-returning-to-study group).

f   Active use of resources. Frances may be encouraged to link up with existing service for women, or to use existing resources creatively (for example, start her own women's group).

g   Social education. Assertiveness training may help Frances feel more comfortable with expressing her own views and needs, and help her link awareness of her views and needs to actively expressing them. This may also decrease both George and Sophia's apparent exploitation of her. Frances may require extra support if her assertiveness at home actually causes more conflict.

Non-radical approach

1 Assessment The main problem seems to be Frances' depression which she calls a 'marriage' problem. Possibly she is more concerned about her marriage than her own emotional well-being. She clearly suffers from low self-esteem, and seems to blame herself for what she sees as past failures in her life. She seems unable to deal with conflict: both the potential conflict with George and Sophia over the issue of Sophia coming to stay, and the conflict about what she should be doing as a good wife and mother. There is certainly some conflict regarding this between the family norms with which Frances was raised and those with which George was raised: Frances' parents expected her to pursue a medical career, George's mother (by example) expected a traditional wifely role.

The marriage itself does not appear to be a particularly strong one. There seems to be little communication between Frances and George, and Frances certainly feels little support from George. The issue of Sophia coming to stay is perceived as both a threat to her marriage, and a threat to her personal happiness: the marriage will end if Sophia does not come to stay; her happiness will end if Sophia does come to stay. She has set an impossible 'no win' situation here, which no doubt causes high stress and related feelings of depression. These conflicts which Frances is unable to deal with, can be readily traced to poor family functioning. There are unclear boundaries between the roles of Frances and Sophia, and there appear to be some inappropriate alliances across generations between Sophia and George. Sophia seems to be identifying with George, and taking on both mother and wife roles. She expects Frances to assume the same responsibility for care of George (and the boys) without the same power. Communication within the family system (certainly between Frances and other family members) is not effective. Frances appears to be scapegoated: the fact that the issue of Sophia coming to live is made out to be mainly Frances' problem, rather than a whole family concern shows this.

That Frances is a very isolated woman contributes to her problem. She gains no support from her husband and appears to have few friends or other family members who might support her. This problem may be exacerbated in the country.

2 *Casework goals* The main aim would be to relieve Frances' feelings of depression by increasing her self-esteem and enabling her to deal with conflict. Family conflicts should also be resolved, and communication between family members improved.

3 *Suggested strategies*
   a   Stress management for Frances.
   b   Personal counselling for Frances to help resolve personal conflicts, raise her self-esteem and provide support.
   c   Marriage guidance counselling for George and Frances to improve communication.
   d   Family therapy to improve family functioning so that Frances is not scapegoated.

CASE 5   AMANDA WEST

Seven-year-old Amanda West attends a program at a special education centre. It is suspected that she has a developmental delay, but she is still undergoing assessment. Amanda and her mother Jean (26) are referred by the educational psychologist at the centre to the centre's social worker to assess whether there might be social reasons for Amanda's developmental delay. Education staff also hint at suspicions of physical abuse—they have often noticed strange bruising on Amanda's arms.

Jean is quite keen for the social worker to visit her at home. She wants to do anything she can for Amanda, agrees with all the professionals so far involved in the case that she has a problem, and blames herself entirely for it. She seems lonely, and is glad to talk about herself and Amanda.

Amanda, Jean and Ken (30), Amanda's father and husband of Jean, live in a working class area of a small city. Ken is a factory shift worker, Jean is engaged in full-time home duties. The house is small and liveable, relatively clean, but not neat or tidy. Jean seems anxious and flustered throughout the social worker's visit, and continues the housework (washing up, ironing) throughout the interview, despite being asked to sit down. Amanda plays quietly in another room. She appears to be a shy, healthy, pretty girl, dressed cleanly and neatly. She does not speak during the social worker's visit. Occasionally, Jean goes to check on her and admonishes her for small things: 'Don't sit like that, you'll crush your dress'. Amanda does not say anything, but will sometimes grunt or whine in apparent frustration.

Jean presents as very concerned about Amanda, but her own intelligence is not high. She appears to manage the housework quite well, but is constantly anxious about it. She says that Ken and his mother Margaret (58) who lives close by, do not think she manages well at all, and blame her for Amanda's problems. She confides that they do have some money worries, but she doesn't understand exactly what they are. She is worried that she may not be a good housewife and mother, as she was brought up in a 'home' (her words). She thinks this might be the reason something is wrong with her, and might be the cause of Amanda's problems.

Jean agrees to some ongoing social work contact to help her with her parenting and to further assess the relationship between mother and daughter. Ken seems uninterested in what Jean does with the social worker, and does not want to be involved in anything. Jean is also referred to a parents' support group run by the special education centre, but the psychologist who runs the group complains that she dominates the conversation with highly personal and inappropriate anecdotes. He is worried that she might ruin the group for the other (mainly middle class) parents, and asks what can be done about her. He thinks that she should no longer attend the group.

Not long after the social worker first meets Jean the special education centre's director informs the social worker that Jean has been suddenly hospitalised by a private psychiatrist. The worker visits Jean in private hospital. Jean is distressed about being there, but does not want to leave because she thinks she cannot cope. It is not clear from Jean what precipitated her hospitalisation except that Ken and Margaret called the psychiatrist because they felt she could not cope. They (and the psychiatrist) claim that Jean had a 'crying fit', and that she was depressed and needed hospitalisation. Margaret is currently looking after Amanda, and prefers to continue doing so until Jean can 'get better fully and be a proper mother'. The psychiatrist is adamant that Jean is depressed (although he does not know why), and that she will require bed-rest for an indefinite period of time. He will not be more specific.

Case plans

Radical approach

1 Assessment There are a number of specific problems which require attention. The first is the problem of Amanda's possible developmental delay, the second that of her potential abuse. Other problems relate more directly to Jean: her involvement with the parent group, and her hospitalisation.

On the information given it is difficult to make a conclusive statement about the causes of Amanda's developmental delay. In social terms, however, it seems feasible to speculate that Jean's own socially disadvantaged background and consequent poor social skills may affect the way she relates to Amanda. This could have some effect on Amanda's behaviour and level of social development. The issue of potential abuse is even more difficult to comment on solely from the information provided. The worker would need to consult further regarding this issue, perhaps seeking more information from Jean and Ken about their treatment of Amanda.

The problem of Jean's behaviour in the group is not entirely Jean's problem. Her behaviour may actually seem quite appropriate to her, given her social background. It seems there may be a clash of class cultures here. Jean fails to understand the group norms which seem to require balanced participation with due attention to other group members, and discretionary self-disclosure. Other group members may not understand the norms Jean is operating from. She seems to assume that self-disclosure, and perhaps self-blame is expected at all costs. There may also be some labelling of Jean as a deviant group member. The psychologist at least seems to do this by assuming that the only solution is that Jean leave the group. It may be his own inability to deal with Jean through normal group processes which is contributing to the problem.

The problem of Jean's hospitalisation is complicated by a number of factors. Firstly, there may be a degree of exploitation on the psychiatrist's (and indirectly on Margaret and Ken's) part. It seems he has not made a clear reasoned diagnosis on the basis of sufficient evidence, nor does he have a clear treatment plan and rationale. One wonders whether Jean's hospitalisation simply suits everyone else's interests. Unfortunately, Jean herself, while not necessarily making the choice to go to hospital, certainly clearly wishes to stay there. This may be partly because she does blame herself and believes in her own inability to cope. In this sense she may be a victim of social labelling. Family and psychiatrist both see her as 'the problem', and Jean has been only too happy to fall in with this view of herself. All participants also subscribe to the dominant, social, mothering role expectations for Jean—the ideological belief appears to be that the mother should bear sole responsibility for the care and satisfactory development of the child. As well, the classic patriarchal model of the non-involved father is reflected by Ken in this family. Another patriarchal symptom is the social conflict, rather than alliance, between the women in the situation: Amanda is a 'victim' because she has a 'problem' which Jean is portrayed as causing, Margaret sides with her son Ken in blaming Jean.

In summary then, we see a situation in which, although there are a number of problems, one person, Jean, seems to be blamed for them all. This appears to be a classic 'blame the victim' situation functioning as preserving the interests of the more powerful parties in the situation—Ken, Margaret, the psychologist and the psychiatrist.

2 Casework goals The main aim would be to ensure Amanda's care and Jean's well-being by equalising power in the situation. This could be done by clarifying role expectations of Jean and challenging any 'false' myths about them.

3 Suggested strategies
a   Active use of resources. This may involve seeking further information about their treatment and care of Amanda from both Jean and Ken whilst empathising with the difficulties of their situation. It may also involve seeking information from the relevant statutory authorities regarding the relative rights of children and parents and obligations of the worker. Jean and Ken may need to be clearly informed of these so they fully understand the possible legal implications of their behaviour and can choose to act accordingly. Provide information about parenting which is empowering; that is, concrete, but capitalising on the positives of their existing practices.
b   Develop critical awareness. Challenge the belief (with Jean, Ken and Margaret separately or together) that Jean is solely responsible for Amanda's 'problem' and her care. Create awareness of the labelling process that has occurred.
c   Empowering techniques. Empower Jean, both through developing her critical awareness (using critical questioning) to

show where her views about herself and her self-blame might come from. Try to reduce her self-blame so that she is freer to make her own choice about staying in the hospital or leaving.

d   Creating alternatives. Create other alternatives for Jean, perhaps through increasing her social support. One solution might be to develop an *alliance* between the women in the situation (Amanda, Jean and Margaret) whereas at present they are conflicting parties. Help Margaret empathise with Jean and Amanda as other women, and get them all to see the commonalities of their situation.

e   Equalise power imbalances. Reduce power imbalances between Jean and the psychologist and psychiatrist respectively. Encourage Jean to ask the psychiatrist specific questions about her diagnosis and treatment plan in order to make him more accountable. Assume the role of advocate on her behalf with the psychologist. Get him to examine group techniques he can use to make the group function better.

f   Bureaucratic techniques. Present Jean's case at a staff case conference playing up the social and structural dimensions of the case and enlisting greater understanding of Jean's situation. Try to devise ways in which other staff can assist Jean; for example, by relating in a more tolerant way, and giving her more concrete suggestions for handling Amanda.

Non-radical approach

1 Assessment The main problem in this situation is the welfare of Amanda. The mother Jean is clearly not coping with her care and requires outside intervention and monitoring to ensure that Amanda's developmental delay is appropriately addressed, and also that Amanda is not abused. Jean is typical of a non-coping mother: depressive, tearful, possibly neurotic in that her own emotional needs are constantly in the forefront. Her own deprived background would probably contribute to this emotional inadequacy. It would also appear that her intelligence is not high, since she cannot seem to understand the purpose of the parent support group. Her own family do not appear to be particularly supportive, so this would contribute to her feelings of inadequacy, but at least they are taking some responsibility by having her hospitalised.

2 Casework goals The main aim should be to ensure the well-being of Amanda.

3 Suggested strategies
   a   Parent education training classes for Jean (and maybe Ken). These may be more appropriate than parent support groups.

b Home help and/or family support for Jean. This will help with the housework and reduce the pressure on Jean.

c Counselling for Jean in order to provide emotional support; also examine the relationship between her own emotional deprivation and her present relationship with Amanda.

d Behavioural techniques to help Jean relate to Amanda in a more positive way.

e Contract statutory authority dealing with child protection and examine the legal implications of the situation. Determine the worker's obligations in the situation and carry them out if necessary.

CASE 6 THE DICKSONS

Terry (25) and Sharon (28) Dickson, and Sharon's two children from a former marriage, Robert (5) and Fiona (4), moved from a large rural town to a large metropolitan city a week ago. On the trip down they were involved in a car accident which meant that Fiona and Sharon had to be hospitalised—Sharon with a fractured pelvis and major bruising, Fiona with a head injury which may affect her eyesight (she is currently undergoing observation and further tests). The Dickson's were referred to a social worker by medical staff because Sharon seems highly anxious about Fiona's condition.

When Sharon is interviewed by the social worker it is discovered that she is mainly anxious because she does not know much about Fiona's diagnosis and treatment, and is also concerned about how Terry and Robert are managing without her. The car was written off in the accident, and although they have salvaged their luggage, they are financially unable to buy another vehicle. Sharon has not been able to see Fiona since the accident because she cannot move with her broken pelvis. Terry is unable to visit much because he is without a car and presently living in a caravan park over two hours' travel (by public transport) from the hospital. Sharon is also worried about how Fiona is coping with being hospitalised, as she is a shy child who has never spent a night away from her mother. She has become even more attached to Sharon since Sharon's divorce from Fiona's father (whom she does not see now) and Sharon's marriage to Terry.

The Dicksons had decided to move for work reasons: after being retrenched from his position in sales with a car firm, Terry had been unemployed for a year and hoped there would be more work in the city. Sharon also planned to find work to help support the family. Now savings are running out and Sharon does not know how long it will be before she is able to work. A further complication is that medical staff wish to discharge Sharon as soon as possible because of bed shortages. She does not know how she will manage living in a caravan park while still on crutches.

Case Plans

Radical approach

1 Assessment From a structural standpoint, the Dicksons are clearly victims of both the economic recession and rural disadvantage. Their recent move was motivated by a need to seek better living opportunities in the city. In an economic downturn, rural areas are often worst hit. Sharon's anxiety about Fiona is entirely understandable given their social circumstances: life changes (marriage break-up and remarriage, and move from country to city); the distressing accident and the nature of Fiona's injuries; and possible lack of information (from medical staff) and support (from medical staff and family). She has possibly been labelled an 'over-protective', problem mother by ward staff. This would need to be checked but, if so, could partly account for staff giving her little information (if this is the case), or perhaps not attempting to allay her anxieties. Sharon's anxiety about Terry and Robert is also understandable given the expected caring roles women perform. The Dickson's entire problem situation is complicated by lack of resources: their finances are low, they have limited means of travel; they are physically separated as a family; they live in a caravan park; and they are threatened by bed shortages in the hospital.

2 Casework goals The first goal would be to alleviate Sharon's anxiety by increasing her power in the hospital situation. The Dicksons may also need assistance coping with the social changes they have been through recently. They may need to be provided with some material resources.

3 Suggested strategies
   a Active use of resources. Provide information to Sharon about Fiona in such a way that will allow her to obtain further information in an ongoing way. For example, ask medical staff to see Sharon and explain Fiona's situation. The social worker could help Sharon ask the questions about which she is most anxious. The worker could encourage Sharon to be assertive in asking these questions in future, and help her learn strategies to deal effectively with medical staff. This would also help increase her power in the hospital situation.
   b Advocacy. Act as advocate for Sharon with medical staff, both in obtaining information about Fiona's condition, and in seeking a longer hospital stay (if that is what Sharon wants).

Reduce any blame staff might direct towards Sharon for her high anxiety level. Make them aware of her difficult social situation (without breaching Sharon's confidentiality).

c Provide material resources. Investigate income security possibilities—empower Terry to do this by helping him actively use these resources, as well as job-finding resources.

d Develop critical awareness. Discuss developments with both Sharon and Terry regarding their current financial situation, so that they do not blame themselves. Also develop critical awareness of how social and economic changes have affected them personally. Show how the changes in social status that Sharon has gone through with her marriages might have affected her relationship with Fiona, expressed in her current anxieties about Fiona's condition and Fiona's attachment to her.

Non-radical approach

1 Assessment The Dickson's main problem is a lack of financial resources which has been exacerbated by their recent move and accident. The mother, Sharon, may be overly anxious about her daughter, Fiona, because of an over-protectiveness developed as a result of her remarriage. Or she may simply be an over-protective mother. Her current sense of isolation is also increased because of the family's lack of resources preventing them seeing each other more regularly. This is a crisis situation, because of the upset to the family system caused by the move from country to city, and also the car accident.

2 Casework goals The main aims would be to provide resources; to allay Sharon's anxiety; and to restore some equilibrium to the family system's normal functioning.

3 Suggested strategies

a Provide suitable material resources such as available benefits, more convenient accommodation, emergency assistance.

b Counselling for Sharon to calm her, help her vent her feelings, reduce her anxiety, perhaps examine the reasons for her anxieties about Fiona.

c Crisis intervention to mobilise the family's normal coping mechanisms.

d Relay information to Sharon from medical staff regarding Fiona's possible diagnosis.

9   Finetuning

Because radical approaches to social work practice with individual people are relatively new, there are still many questions of fine-tuning. On the face of it, there are many obvious practical limitations to the practice of radical casework and many ethical and theoretical questions which need to be clarified so that workers can proceed less ambiguously. For example, is there any difference between politicising clients (as discussed in chapter 7 in relation to developing critical awareness) and practising from a radical perspective with them? Are radical and feminist approaches appropriate for work with all types of client groups? Is there an inherent class bias in the use of structural and gender analysis? These are questions often raised by caseworkers who wish to practise radically, but cannot see past the very real limitations of the day-to-day work places or clientele.

LIMITATIONS ON RADICAL CASEWORK PRACTICE

One of the major limitations in the practice of radical casework may relate to the particular person's being helped and to the situation. Where does the person who is being helped actually fit in a radical practice model? What are the roles and rights? What power does the person command in the helping context? What choices are had about helping and being helped?

First we need to reiterate that a radical perspective always assumes *equality* between the professional and the person being helped.

Because personal liberation is valued, diminishing the power differences between the worker and client is an implicit goal. Central to this is the underlying ethic of self-determination, a principle upheld in traditional social work, and reaffirmed and given more prominence by a radical perspective. But how much self-determination does a person really have when the worker is using a radical perspective?

There is always some ambiguity over the ethic of self-determination when trying to intervene to change a situation. This has been well acknowledged by traditional social work theorists, and applies equally to change sought by radicals. It is logically impossible, for instance, for two people to work together for change without some imposition and exchange of values (Pincus & Minahan, 1973:43). The worker therefore will most likely influence the person being helped in some way and, therefore, it would not be true to say that the client has been purely self-determining.

Secondly, there are social, moral and material limitations on the extent to which an individual person can be self-directing. Other people in the person's life (including the worker) have a right not to be harmed by any action taken by him or her, as does society at large. The individual's choices may not be in harmony with those of the larger society, particularly as embodied in legal, economic or political structures (Bernstein, 1960). There may not be the resources to take the path chosen.

Thirdly, there may be limitations special to the people themselves. They may not know what they want, or may choose *not* to choose for themselves. This might be the case with people who are not used to exercising their own choice; for instance, a person with disabilities who has been deliberately disempowered. People may be ambivalent, or unclear about what they want, or just not have the capacity for decision making. Unfortunately some of the goals of radical casework (such as personal autonomy) assume a desire for and ability to obtain that goal. In cases where the person is unsure about what is wanted and, depending on the context of the worker's brief, the worker may need to help the person learn some decision making skills, or simply learn to exercise choices within the imitations which already exist. It may be, of course, that some of these self-limitations will dissolve if the worker focuses on empowering the person.

Should a person be allowed to choose not to make a choice, or not to be self-determining? It is difficult to address this question unequivocally, since there may conceivably be situations where such a course might override the other considerations, when quick action must be taken and the client does not have the necessary capacities to make a quick decision. There are, of course, other reasons people may choose not to be self-determining. They may believe themselves to be incapable, they may believe it is the responsibility of the worker to direct them, they may not wish to assume responsibility for their own decisions, they may be fearful of making their own choice. However, in principle it would seem that if taking a radical perspective, self-determination is assumed. If people choose not to make their own choices after all the possible reasons for this self-limitation have been addressed, it may have to be concluded that their belief system is incompatible with a radical approach, and some other perspective adopted.

Yet another limitation on the radical approach may be simply that of disagreement between the person and his or her worker. Disagreements might particularly occur over political interpretation, since the political assumptions of a radical approach are much more explicit than with traditional perspectives. They are, therefore, potentially more threatening. Even if people agree with the radical worker's interpretation of the situation they may be reluctant to follow through with this approach if it means major upheavals in their private life. This is not exclusive to radical practice. Change per se can be threatening, and workers often experience frustration with people who choose not to change their situations, but to return to their problems, simply because that is what they are used to. It may, therefore, be necessary for radical workers to assist people to cope with change.

Clients have a right to disagree with their caseworker. If reasons for the disagreement have been explored and if the disagreement is unresolvable, clients also have the right not to be politicised, since the primary aim of radical casework is to help people, not to politicise them. Often, of course, the two processes are inseparable, but where a person perceives that they are being politicised at the expense of being helped, it may be the point at which the radical worker should adopt a more traditional approach, or at least a less explicitly radical one. I am not suggesting here that a worker should be, for example, knowingly sexist, but simply that in such cases it might be more acceptable to some clients to concentrate on their personal feelings, for instance, rather than the social or political reasons for their situation.

As well as the right to disagree, clients also have the right to fail (Soyer, 1963). This right is implicit in the right to choose one's path in life. Clients are not obliged to succeed in order to please their caseworkers. However, although we need to respect personal choice, Soyer (1963:72) points out social workers should guard against being too conservative in the name of reality. Workers and clients may be in danger of setting goals that are too low, assuming that 'reality' cannot be changed. This very assumption can, of course, prevent change happening. On the other hand, people may be encouraged to try for more challenging goals if these goals are actually set. Clients also have the right to learn the limits of their reality for themselves.

How does the radical caseworker deal with all these personal and social limitations, which may stand in the way of broader ranging personal and social change? First, as Galper (1980:149) points out, we need to begin with the traditional social work adage of 'starting where the client is at':

> We need to start, as social workers have known for some time, where people are, on the issues they experience as most pressing in their lives and on ground they can understand. When people come to agencies with pressing immediate problems, we must help them to deal with those problems. It may be that a person under great psychological stress simply cannot develop a larger perspective on that distress unless and until she or he experiences symptomatic relief.

Having begun where the person is at, the radical caseworker and client then need to examine together the nature of the limitations which stand in the way of achieving personal autonomy and change. The radical principle should always be to minimise these limitations, not to accept at face value that they cannot be changed. The essence of personal liberation in this sense is to accept that socially determined limitations need *not* necessarily be personal ones. If, on closer examination, it is decided that this limitations must be accepted, the goal should be to maximise personal choices within or around these boundaries.

RADICAL PRACTICE WITH INVOLUNTARY CLIENTS

The second obvious area of limitation to radical practice is with public welfare or involuntary clients. Social workers are often openly employed as 'agents of social control', typically in corrective, protective, institutional and bureaucratic settings. It seems paradoxical to claim that it is possible to encourage personal liberation in these types of settings, where the worker's main role may be to supervise, monitor or regulate behaviour which is viewed as socially undesirable. Unfortunately there is not enough specific work done on radical practice in these settings, although some work is now beginning to emerge on empowerment in public child welfare settings (Hegar & Hunzeker, 1988). Ironically, it may be that a radical perspective carries most potency in these fields of work because it is here that social limitations and their potentially detrimental effect on individual people is most obvious. Radical caseworkers may be able to concentrate public attention on the undesirable behaviour of clients which is clearly worsened by the undesirable aspects of these institutions. The institutionalised behaviour of residents who have been incarcerated for long periods is one example which has gained much recent attention with the widespread moves towards de-institutionalisation. Maximising information to clients, and thereby maximising their choices within a restricted situation, can give clients some autonomy. Decreasing self-blame by alerting people to the political and social reasons for certain imposed limitations can also be potentially liberating. This includes workers being honest about their own personal, social and political interests in the given situation, so that clients can take these into account in their decision making. Barber's (1991) model of 'negotiated casework' picks up on some of these issues in more detail. His framework encourages the worker to be clear about what is and what is not negotiable, and then to negotiate as far as possible within these boundaries.

RADICAL WORK IN A NON-RADICAL SETTING?

Is it possible to work from a radical and feminist perspective using structures and procedures which are sexist or exploitative, or with colleagues and supervisors who do not agree with (or simply do not understand) feminist or radical assumptions? Much radical work may actually be beyond the brief of particular agencies, or beyond the role of a particular casework in a particular agency. It is tempting when working in a setting which seems completely antithetical to a feminist or radical perspective to simply acquiesce to it, believing that a radical approach calls for broad changes and that no structural good will be served by trying to reform the existing system on the small scale. Unfortunately, if we think this way, many dehumanising and disempowering practices which presently exist will continue to flourish. It is *preferable*, therefore, if working from a radical perspective in a non-radical setting, to attempt to radicalise that setting in some way. The politics of 'the unfinished', which I discussed in chapter 7, is a useful stance to take if presented with a situation like this. From this stance, small-scale changes are viewed as a vital part of the large-scale, still as yet 'unfinished' social change which is aimed for. Small-scale changes are, therefore, important and should not be devalued simply because they are not large-scale changes. All change in this sense is valuable, as long as small-scale change does not become a substitution for large-scale change and thereby function to deflect structural changes which still need to be made.

Even if small-scale changes are preferable to no changes in a non-radical or sexist setting, are they *possible*? To the extent that social workers are supposed to be autonomous self-directing professionals, the answer is yes. We all have some discretion, even in the most controlled settings, about how we actually relate on an interpersonal level with clients. Thus interpersonally we can relate in as equal as possible, and in as empowering a manner as possible. We can empathise with and analyse clients' situations so that they are not blamed for structural causes of their problems. We can suggest creative alternatives for them, and put them in touch with these when they fall outside the bounds of our own areas. We can change and redesign restrictive agency practices, and we can challenge sexist or victim-blaming attitudes from our own colleagues. We can emphasise the benefits of the feminist movement and non-sexist analysis for men and children. Dominelli and McLeod (1989) cover this issue briefly, and also look more closely at ways in which a feminist political presence can be established. Some form of radical or feminist practice is possible on some level in all agency settings.

POLITICISING CLIENTS

Is radical casework simply politicising clients? The answer to this question is both yes and no. Yes in the sense that all social work, be it traditional, conservative, feminist, radical or whatever, is a form of politicisation in that every set of ideas on which we base our practice has an implicit political base. In radical and feminist perspectives, however, the politics are not mainstream, and are therefore more obvious. But as Galper says so well, 'Radicals do not seek to introduce politics to an apolitical situation. Rather we mean to challenge the politics of compliance, and to introduce the politics of resistance and change' (1980:11).

However, just because casework help, conservative or radical, is inherently political, does not mean that helping clients is the same as actively seeking to politicise them. *Personal help is the primary goal of casework, whether it is conservatively or radically practised.* In some instances it may be that the active politicisation of a person is expressly helpful. This might be the case, say, with a newly divorced woman who blames herself for her marriage breakdown and cannot accept her single state. Her self-esteem might be increased and her stress lowered if she can see patriarchal reasons why her marriage ended, and can learn that singleness should not be a socially stigmatised state.

There may be other sorts of situations where politicisation is helpful, but should remain less explicit; for example, a family trying to make a decision about whether to place ageing parents in nursing home care may be partially helped by realising that their difficult choice is not entirely their fault. The fact that there are few socially sanctioned viable options for care of the elderly complicates their decision. It may not be helpful, however, to concentrate their attentions on this inadequate social response to the elderly, since it may only increase their feelings of despair for their own situation. Instead, it may be better to focus on the options for care of their parents, and to deal with the social reasons for their grief or guilt as these arise.

WHO IS RADICAL WORK APPROPRIATE FOR?

At first glance it would appear that radical and feminist perspectives are most strongly applicable to socially disadvantaged groups (low income groups, the aged, youth, women, ethnic and racial minorities, people with disabilities, sexually deviant groups, rural dwellers). This is, however, at best a superficial appreciation of the social analysis used by radicals and feminists, which is fundamentally an understanding of how *all* groups in society are socially determined (although not necessarily oppressed). Radical (and feminist) analysis provides a particularly succinct understanding of the ways in which *all* groups contribute to the disadvantage of *some*. All groups, oppressed and oppressors, actually take on roles and beliefs, and build structures which maintain existing inequalities. This analysis, therefore, is in theory applicable to all potential client groups. Feminists too are beginning to recognise the relevance of their analysis to work with men (Dominelli & McLeod, 1989:95–6) in so far as men are also trapped in particular sex-role stereotypes which can be detrimental to their emotional needs. However, more work needs to be done regarding radical and feminist strategies with groups which are not traditionally regarded as powerless.

There is another group which may be less amenable to a purely radical approach. We touched on the issue in chapter 5, when we examined ways of categorising problem types. There I suggested that where the purely personal aspects of the problem were predominant, more traditional counselling techniques might be more appropriate. These traditional techniques can still be subsumed under a radical approach, of course, provided that their use does not disempower clients, or blame them for problems which are essentially socially caused. Examples might be cases of severe crisis or disaster, where immediate physical and emotional needs must be addressed. Other situations involving grief, loss or bereavement, such as divorce, death, job loss, sudden illness or disability, may need to be initially handled in this way. In cases of change and adjustment to change or transition such as with migration and settlement, or retirement, similar needs may require initial attention. In the longer term structural aspects may assume more importance, and may need to be handled accordingly at the time. This naturally depends on the brief of the caseworker within the particular agency setting—which may not include longer term work. Recommendations, however, can still be made regarding longer term case plans for the person.

There may be other groups of people for whom radical or feminist perspectives are a total anathema. Rural dwellers, although disadvantaged, might fall into this group as a traditionally conservative population. This does not necessarily mean that radical perspectives are irrelevant and inappropriate for them. Indeed, because they are disadvantaged socially and economically, radical perspectives are particularly applicable. Feminism is particularly applicable to a large sector of country women (Alston, 1990) possibly because of the undoubted economic role women on the farm perform. All this means that radical or feminist work may need to be approached in a particular way if working in the country (Fook & Colingridge, 1988; Alston, 1990). Care may need to be taken that the ideas are not perceived as too threatening, and that the analysis is clearly applicable to the rural person's everyday situation.

The same qualification can be made regarding people from more traditional cultures where conservative political views are more acceptable. For example, the plight of women in developing countries is particularly delicate given that the social position of women is often far behind that of their counterparts in other countries. However, women (and men) from these countries may have particular difficulty in accepting, for example, Australian laws regarding domestic violence. This leads us to the next doubt about radical and feminist approaches: not only that they are essentially urban biased, but they are also class and culturally biased, and are, therefore, not really applicable to the bulk of social work clientele.

MIDDLE CLASS BIAS

Is there an inherent middle class bias in radical and feminist perspectives? The answer is undoubtedly yes. But so there is in the whole social work profession. Let us not fool ourselves here. The whole industry of social work—the people it recruits, accreditation

standards and requirements, tertiary level education, job organisation, cultural bias in treatment methodologies, analysis of social
problems, professional status, pay levels, professional subculture—
all are middle class. This is a fact of our present social system. Our
ideas, be they radical, feminist or traditional, originate from the
middle class, because academic occupations are middle class occupations. However, just because they are middle class does not mean
they are not applicable to other classes. The use of a theory should
be judged by its ability to explain the complexities of our world. If
radical and feminist theories can explain the social struggle of
people, whether middle or working class, then they have value.
Since many of our efforts for change with our working class clients
are aimed at giving working class people what the middle classes
are lucky enough to take more for granted—resources, decision-
making power, social mobility, education, more choices in life, a
better standard of living, access to services—it is not contradictory
that we try to teach them some middle class beliefs about themselves
and ways of doing things, in order to achieve these goals.

CULTURAL BIAS

There are, however, some elements of potential middle class and
cultural bias in some of the assumptions and strategies of a radical
approach which may render aspects of it inapplicable or at least
difficult to apply across classes or cultures. Radical and feminist
casework, for instance, places a high value on individualism and
independence (such as embodied in the ethics of self-determination
or the goal of personal autonomy and liberation). These sorts of
assumptions may not be shared across cultures (Pedersen, 1987).
Some cultures may place a higher importance on community responsibility and inter-dependence.

Relationship to authority can vary between classes and cultures
as well. Some classes and cultures may be highly suspicious of
authority as represented by the social worker, in which case a radical
worker's best intentions to empower the client from a different class
or cultural background may not be believed by that person.

There is a similar problem regarding communication differences.
It is generally acknowledged that there are communication differences between cultures (for example, Nguyen, 1991), and also
subcultural differences between genders (Holmes, 1985). There may
even be differences among Western cultures (for example, between
America and Australia) regarding communication principles (Fook,
1989b:95). Given that these differences exist, the radical caseworker
needs to be careful about too uncritically adopting micro-counselling

techniques, as expounded by authors such as Ivey (1989), since this approach is largely American and middle class based. In fact an uncritical adoption of micro-counselling techniques may actually be antithetical to radical and feminist approaches because it downplays the importance of social and structural context, and may function to support conservative social beliefs (Fook, 1989b). Gender analysis of communication patterns has indicated that there are differences between the way gender groups communicate, in which case radical caseworkers should perhaps be looking to develop gender-appropriate styles of communication. Micro-counselling, with the particular emphasis on empathy and verbalisation of feelings, may be more suitable to feminine communication styles. There may be different forms of help which are more suitable to men (McHugh, 1990), and which require further development into the radical caseworker's repertoire.

WHERE DO WE GO FROM HERE?

It has been my hope that by specifying particular strategies for radical casework practice, and showing in detail how they are derived directly from radical and feminist analysis, and traditional practice, it will be easier for those who wish to conscientiously practice casework radically. There is a long road yet to travel, and it is not dissimilar to that travelled by all well-intentioned professionals. The questions of whether, how and why our practice is effective are still largely unanswered for radical and feminist caseworkers, although work has begun in the area. In this, however, we are little different from our more traditional colleagues when it comes to research which can claim to prove or disprove the effectiveness of a particular approach. Research which does exist tends to concentrate on measuring the effectiveness of a particular program (for example, Rubin, 1985), rather than of entire theories of practice. As yet, therefore, we are not really in a position to draw final conclusions about the relative effectiveness of different theoretical perspectives, although we are often rightly committed to different approaches. What is needed from here is for radical and feminist caseworkers, like their counterparts following different perspectives, to document and test their own specific initiatives, in particular situations. I hope this book has made the theory base of radical casework practice clearer, so that as we continue to test specific practices, we will thereby contribute to the more ambitious tasks of refining our broad approach to radical casework practice.

Appendix I: Assessment guide

This may be used in conjunction with discussion in chapter 5. It is a checklist of factors which the caseworker may find useful to note in assessing the client's situation.

MATERIAL OR PHYSICAL ASPECTS

- General presentation and appearance
- General health or medical state; for example, age, disability, illness
- Housing situation; for example, type of housing, members of household, who owns it
- Broad financial position; for example, type and level of income
- Major family and life events and history

PSYCHOLOGICAL ASPECTS

- General intellectual ability and awareness; ability to verbalise
- Self-image: how does the person see him or herself, personal goals and roles he or she plays?
- Self-esteem: how does the person value him or herself, for example, how confident is he or she?
- Motivation: what might be the person's reasons (other than the stated ones) for engaging with the social worker? How committed is he or she to change?
- Coping mechanisms; for example, how does the person rationalise her

or his situation? Does she or he project anxieties? Does she or he deny aspects of the problem situation?

* General emotional and behavioural level: does the person appear overly anxious, depressed, frustrated, angry or unconcerned?
* Life changes: how she or he has coped with perceived changes throughout life; for example, losses, transitions, changes in status, stages in life?
* Perceptions of the problem situation: what is the person's own view of the situation?
* How much choice or power has the person in life?

SOCIAL ASPECTS

* What close relationships the person has
* Any significant power relationships in the person's life
* How they relate to family, peers, close friends, neighbours, marriage partner, etc.; for example, who do they see regularly?
* What social groups do they belong to; for example, clubs, church groups, youth gangs
* What social roles do they play; for example, parent, loving sister, breadwinner, neighbourhood helper
* How they use their leisure time
* General social support system: from where do they draw their main emotional and social support; for example, from marriage partner, pets, day centre
* Work or occupation
* Social changes through life; for example, occupational changes, marriage breakdown, moving or migration

STRUCTURAL ASPECTS

* Socio-economic class: what values, ways of relating, range of experiences does the person have as a result of her or his past and present class? Is their present class different from a past one? Are there any difficulties resulting from this?
* Gender: how the person's gender has influenced her or his past and present life.
* Does the person bear any particular social labels; for example, 'pensioner', 'migrant', 'unemployed'. Is he or she stigmatised as a result?
* Religion: what values she or he holds as a result of a particular religious upbringing; what importance this plays in her or his life?
* Culture and ethnicity: what is her or his cultural background? Is she or he part of a racial or cultural or ethnic minority group? How important is this in her or his life? Are there problems resulting from this?

- Subculture: does the person belong to any subcultures which might have a particular influence on her or his situation; for example, drug or criminal subculture, youth subculture?
- Occupation and education level: are they congruent? Is the person satisfied with these? Does the person hold any particular status or professional values?
- Relationships with social institutions (past or present); for example, legal offences, school refusal?
- Socially held beliefs and 'myths': how do these affect the person and her or his situation?
- Structural changes throughout her or his life; for example, class, culture
- Influence of the particular cultural or political climate in the person's past or present experience

Appendix II: Social self-awareness exercise

This exercise can be done individually or in a small group setting. The aim of this is to try to identify who you are socially, and to increase your awareness from this, of how the social structure influences and has influenced who you are today.

1   Draw up a list of social structures, or aspects of the social structure which you think have influenced your life choices in some way. The list might include:

- marital status
- occupation
- social class (past and present)
- education
- family type and background
- ethnicity
- nationality
- racial background
- religion
- membership of groups or subcultures
- gender
- sexual orientation
- health
- age
- particular historical period (past and/or present)
- social labels
- particular ideologies

2 Try to identify who you are socially by locating yourself against each of these items.
3 Then think about how each of them influences/has influenced your life.

Following is a hypothetical example of how a typical Australian social work student might respond.

STEPS 1 AND 2

marital status	divorced and remarried
occupation	full-time student, home duties
social class	middle middle (present) lower middle (past)
education	studying towards second degree (already have BA)
family type	family of origin traditional nuclear family; at present nuclear family but not traditional (?): two children (son 21, daughter, 20) from first marriage
ethnicity	Australian Italian (parents born Italy)
nationality	Australian
racial background	Italian (?—not sure about this)
religion	raised as Catholic, no religion at present
groups or subcultures	belong to local 'green' collective
gender	female
sexual orientation	heterosexual
health	slight disability—walk with aid of stick as result of car accident
age	41
historical periods	influenced by 1960s and 1970s as young person; influenced by the women's movement
social labels	'just a housewife'; 'professional student'; 'greenie'

| ideologies | green movement; feminism (?); social justice |

STEP 3

How have these influenced who and what I am today? The particular historical period in which I grew up and now find myself as a woman probably means that I was encouraged to marry and have children early (when 19 years old—my cultural background also had a role here). The fact that I have returned to study as a mature age student has something to do with the changing roles of women. Although I don't think I am a feminist, I am very interested in what these women have to say because I think they have made things a lot easier for girls growing up today than they were in my day. I became involved in the 'green' movement because my children became very interested in it during their schooling. I think I have a fairly good sense of what it is like to be 'different' socially, because I grew up as an Italian child in the days before multi-culturalism became popular. Now I find that the fact I have a slight disability sometimes means people relate to me in a more patronising way than they did before I had the accident. It has made me really aware how easily people can label because of superficial appearances, and relate to you on that basis. It makes me readier to prove myself I think.

I have also become more aware of social class differences because I have been slightly socially mobile. My father, as a new migrant, worked several factory jobs and later started his own small business. I am now firmly middle class in that I have an education and my present husband is an architect. These social changes I have gone through have helped to make me aware of how society can determine who and what people are. For example, I don't think I would be studying social work now if I had been born ten years earlier, or if my husband wasn't a professional, or if I hadn't had the car accident. These particular social circumstances have given me this interest in social justice, and the opportunity to study and do something about it.

QUESTIONS FOR DISCUSSION

- Which factors are more important?
- How important have they been in determining who you are today, and the present situation in which you find yourself (for example, studying social work)? Are there any particular beliefs, expectations, rules or

restrictions which resulted from these social structures which have directly affected you personally?
- What particular labels were used in trying to define yourself socially?
- How were these labels defined?
- What beliefs do they reflect about what is socially normal or desirable?
- What are some more purely personal factors which have influenced your life? How do these interact with structural factors?

Appendix III: Using social self-awareness in work with clients

After constructing your own social–structural identity, repeat the process for an individual in a particular case example (choose one from chapter 8). Now compare your profile with the case study's point by point, noting the similarities and differences. How do you feel about working with a person of this social type? How might each of these similarities or differences influence:

- your perceptions of each other
- the assumptions you might make about each other
- your mutual expectations
- the way you communicate or relate to each other
- the types of strategies you might suggest

Would you work differently with someone who is socially similar to you than you would with someone who is socially dissimilar?

Appendix IV: Social empathy exercise

Bob (53) is seeking assistance for stress management after his divorce:

> My wife left because she said I'm boring. I've tried to be a good husband and provider, but it's hard to know what women want these days. They probably don't even know. Now I can't sleep at nights because I lie awake thinking none of it's been worth it—the house, the car, the extra study at nights. Here I am a top professional man as well, and that's not enough for women.

1 What are Bob's *personal* concerns in this extract?
2 What are his *social* concerns?
3 How would you respond empathically to Bob's personal concerns?
4 How would you respond empathically to his social concerns?
5 How would you respond empathically to both his personal and social concerns?

POSSIBLE ANSWERS

1 Bob seems puzzled that he hasn't measured up to his wife's expectations. He seems in two minds about whether this is his fault, the fault of his wife, or the fault of women generally for not being clear about what they want. He is starting to question his life achievements which is causing a great deal of stress.
2 Bob is worried about the current social expectations women

161

place on men. He is implying that women want too much or that what they want is unrealistic, or that they are unclear about it (and, therefore, unfair). They should perhaps be satisfied with the house, car and successful husband, although he is unsure about this. He is also not sure whether he should be satisfied with the general trappings of social success.

3 To Bob: 'You're bewildered by the fact that your own and your wife's expectations don't seem to have measured up, and it seems to be really stressing you out, and making you question everything you've striven for up till now.'

4 To Bob: 'You think that women's current social expectations of men may be unfair?' Or: 'You think the social standards you've always set for yourself should be good enough for women generally?'

5 To Bob: 'You seem quite bewildered by both your wife's and women's general expectations of a husband, and the fact that it's caused you to doubt the worth of your achievements.'

OTHER STATEMENTS WHICH MAY BE USED FOR THIS EXERCISE

Elderly woman in nursing home:

I feel terrible. Just lying here all the time while others come and go. And when I want anything I have to ask someone else to get it for me. Why does it have to be like that for us?

Unemployed man:

Things get horribly bad sometimes, but I never let them get me down. After all, if I give up, what will the family think?

Woman, talking about what is happening in her workplace:

I never get a say in what goes on. Sure they ask me my opinion, but they'll turn around and do the opposite the next day. Maybe my opinion doesn't really count, as a woman. I don't know why they bother to ask; I don't think I'll bother to answer next time.

References

Agel, R. 1971, *The Radical Therapist*, Ballantine, New York

Albury, R. 1976, 'Ideology: the origin of the term', *Tharunka*, 13 October, pp.3–4

Alfrero, L.A. 1972,' Conscientisation', *New Themes in Social Work Education*, International Association of Schools of Social Work, New York

Alston, M. 1990, 'Feminism and farm women', *Australian Social Work*, vol. 43, no. 1, pp.23–7

Alinsky, S. 1971, *Rules for Radicals*, Vintage, New York

Armstrong, J. and Gill, K. 1978, 'The unitary approach: what relevance for community work?', *Social Work Today* vol. 10, no. 11, November, pp. 18–21

Bailey, R. and Brake, M. eds 1975, *Radical Social Work*, Edward Arnold, London

——1980, *Radical Social Work and Practice*, Edward Arnold, London

Barber, J. 1988, 'Are microskills worth teaching?', *Journal of Social Work Education*, no. 1, pp. 3–12

——1991, *Beyond Casework*, Macmillan, London

Barbour, R.S. 1984, 'Social work education—tackling the theory–practice dilemma', *British Journal of Social Work*, vol. 14, pp. 557–77.

Bartlett, H.M. 1970, *The Common Base of Social Work Practice*, National Association of Social Workers, New York

Beecher, S. 1986, 'A gender critique of family therapy' *Gender Reclaimed*, eds H. Marchant and B. Wearing, Hale & Iremonger, Sydney, pp. 64–79

Berlin, S. and Kravetz, D. 1981, 'Women as victims: a feminist social work perspective', *Social Work*, pp. 447–9

Bernstein, S. 1960, 'Self-determination: king or citizen in the realm of values?', *Social Work*, vol. 5, no. 1, pp. 3–8

163

Biestek, F. P. 1957, *The Casework Relationship*, George Allen & Unwin, London

Bolger, S., Corrigan, P., Docking, J. and Frost, N. 1981, *Towards Socialist Welfare Work*, Macmillan, London

Bouchier, D. 1983, *The Feminist Challenge*, Macmillan, London

Bowers, S. 1949, 'The nature and definition of social casework: part III' *Journal of Social Casework*, December, pp. 412–17

Brennan, T. and Parker, N. 1966, *The Foundations of Social Casework*, Ian Novak, Sydney

Briar, S. and Miller, H. 1971, *Problems and Issues in Social Casework*, Columbia University Press, New York & London

Bricker-Jenkins, M. and Hooyman, N. R. 1986, 'A feminist world view: ideological themes from the feminist movement', *Not for Women Only*, eds M. Bricker-Jenkins and N.R. Hooyman, National Association of Social Work, New York

Brodsky, A. M. 1980, 'Therapeutic aspects of consciousness-raising groups', *Alternative Social Services for Women*, ed. N. Gottlieb, Columbia University Press, New York

Brook, E. and Davis, A. eds 1985, *Women, the Family and Social Work*, Tavistock, London & New York

Brown, M. A. G. 1966, 'A review of casework methods', *New Developments in Casework*, ed. E. Younghusband, George Allen & Unwin, London

Bruno, F. J. 1957, *Trends in Social Work 1874–1956*, Columbia University Press, New York & London

Bryson, L. 1977, 'Poverty Research in the Seventies: Unmasking Noble Terms', *Australian & New Zealand Journal of Sociology*, vol. 13, and no. 3, pp. 196–202

Callan, V. 1985, *Choices About Children*, Longman Cheshire, Melbourne

Carkhuff, R. R. and Berenson, B. G. 1977, *Beyond Counselling and Therapy*, Holt, Rinehart & Winston, New York

Carr, E. H. 1961, *What is History?*, Penguin, Harmondsworth

Chamberlain, E. 1975, 'Value dilemmas in old and new methods of social work', *Australian Social Work*, vol. 28, no. 1, pp. 5–13

——ed. 1988, *Change and Continuity in Australian Social Work*, Longman Cheshire, Sydney

Clapton, G. 1977, 'Radicalism—what does it all add up to?', *Social Work Today*, vol. 8, no. 28, p. 16

Clarke, M. 1976, 'The limits of radical social work', *British Journal of Social Work*, vol. 6, no. 4, pp. 504–5

Cohen, S. 1975, 'It's all right for you talk: political and sociological manifestos for social action', *Radical Social Work*, eds R. Bailey and M. Brake, Edward Arnold, London

Coleman, J. V. 1950, 'Distinguishing between psychotherapy and case-work', *Techniques and Principles of Social Casework (1940–1950)*, ed. C. Kasius, Greenwood, Connecticut

Compton, B. R. and Galaway, B. 1989, *Social Work Processes*, Dorsey, Illinois

Considine, M. 1978, 'The death and resurrection of conservative ideology:

Australian social work in the seventies', *Social Alternatives*, vol. 1, no. 2, pp. 50–4

Cornwell, M. 1976, 'Developments in Social Casework since 1965', *Social Work in Australia*, eds P. Boas and J. Crawley, Australian International Press & Publishing, Sydney

Corrigan, P. and Leonard, P. 1978, *Social Work Practice under Capitalism: A Marxist Approach*, Macmillan, London

Cowger, C. D. and Atherton, C. R. 1977, 'Social control: A rationale for social welfare', *Welfare in Action*, eds P. Halmos et al., Routledge & Kegan Paul, London

Crawley, J. 1989, 'Marital casework: option or necessity?', *Australian Social Work*, vol, no. 1, pp. 3–13

Davies, B. 1982, 'Towards a "personalist" framework for radical social work education', *Theory and Practice in Social Work*, eds R. Bailey and P. Lee, Basil Blackwell, Oxford

Dominelli, L. and McLeod, E. 1989, *Feminist Social Work*, Macmillan, London

Egan, G. 1982, *The Skilled Helper*, Brooks & Cole, Monterey

Eisenstein, H. 1984, *Contemporary Feminist Thought*, Unwin Paperbacks, London

Fischer, J. 1976, *The Effectiveness of Social Casework*, Charles C. Thomas, Illinois

Fook, J. 1984, 'Practice principles from life span studies', *Welfare in Australia*, Winter, pp. 22–7

——1986, 'Feminist contributions to casework practice', *Gender Reclaimed: Women in Social Work*, eds H. Marchant and B. Wearing, Hale & Iremonger, Sydney

——1987, 'Structural perspectives in casework: can they guide practice?' *Australian Social Work*, vol. 40, no. 4, pp. 43–4

——1988, 'Teaching casework: incorporating radical and feminist perspectives in the current curriculum', *Advances in Social Welfare Education*, eds R. Berreen et al., University of New South Wales, Kensington

——1989a, 'New directions for social casework', *Australian Social Work*, vol. 42, no. 2 pp. 42–3

——1989b, 'Teaching casework: incorporating radical and feminist perspectives in the current curriculum part II' *Advances in Social Welfare Education*, eds D. James and T. Vinson, University of New South Wales, Kensington

——1990a, 'Australian rural social work in the 1990s' *Australian Social Work*, vol. 43, no. 1, pp. 2–3

——1990b, 'Radical social casework: linking theory and practice' *Social Change and Social Welfare Practice*, eds J. Petruchenia and R. Thorpe, Hale & Iremonger, Sydney

——1991, 'Interest in radical social work today', *Australian Social Work*, vol. 44, no. 1, p. 2

Fook, J. and Collingridge, M. 1988, 'Teaching rural social work and welfare', *Australian Association of Social Workers Newsletter (NSW) Branch*, no. 3, pp. 18–20

Foren, R. and Bailey, R. 1968, *Authority in Social Casework*, Pergamon, London

Freire, P. 1972, *Pedagogy of the Oppressed*, Penguin, Harmondsworth

Furlong, M. 1987, 'A rationale for the use of empowerment as a goal in casework', *Australian Social Work*, vol. 40, no. 3, pp. 25–30

Gambrill, E. 1983, *Casework: A Competency-based Approach*, Prentice-Hall, New Jersey

Galper, J.H. 1975, *The Politics of the Social Services*, Prentice-Hall, New Jersey

———1980, *Social Work Practice: A Radical Perspective*, Prentice-Hall, New Jersey

Germain, C. and Gitterman, A. 1980, *The Life Model of Social Work Practice*, Columbia University Press, New York

Gilbert, L. A. 1980, 'Feminist therapy', *Women and Psychotherapy*, eds A. M. Brodsky and R. T. Hare-Mustin, Guilford Press, New York, pp. 245–65

Goffman, E. 1963, *Stigma*, Penguin, Harmondsworth

Goldberg, G. 1974, 'Structural approach to practice: a new model', *Social Work*, pp. 150–5

Goldberg, G. and Elliot, J. 1980, 'Below the belt: situational ethics for unethical situations', *Journal of Sociology and Social Welfare*, vol. 7, nos 4–6, pp. 478–86

Gottlieb, N. 1980, 'Women and mental health: the problem of depression', *Alterative Social Services for Women*, ed. N. Gottlieb, Columbia University Press, New York

Hain, P. 1975, *Radical Regeneration*, Quartet, London

Halmos, P. 1965, *The Faith of the Counsellors*, Constable, London

Hamilton, G. 1950, 'The underlying philosophy of social casework', *Principles and Techniques in Social Casework (1940–1950)*, ed. C. Kasius, Greenwood Press, Connecticut

———1951, *Theory and Practice of Social Casework*, Columbia University Press, New York & London

Hanisch, C. 1971, 'The personal is political', *The Radical Therapist*, ed. J. Agel, Ballantine, New York

Hart, N. 1976, *When Marriage Ends*, Tavistock, London

Healy, B. 1991, Can social work be radical?, unpub.

Hearn, G. 1985, 'Patriarchy, professionalisation and the semi-professions', *Women and Social Policy*, ed. C. Ungerson, Macmillan, Basingstoke

Hegar, R. L. and Hunzeker, J. M. 1988, 'Moving towards empowerment-based practice in child public welfare', *Social Work*, pp. 499–502

Hepworth, D. H. and Larsen, J. A. 1982, *Direct Social Work Practice: Theory and Skills*, Dorsey, Illinois

Hollis, F. 1964, *Casework: A Psychosocial Therapy*, Random House, New York

———1980, 'On revisiting social work', *Social Casework*, vol. 61, no. 1, January, pp. 3–10

Holmes, J. 1985, 'Sex differences and miscommunication', *Cross Cultural Encounters*, ed. J. B. Pride, River Seine, Melbourne

Howe, D. 1987, *An Introduction to Social Work Theory*, Wildwood House, London

Huber, R. 1984, 'People of the Mediterranean', *Communication and Cultural Diversity and the Health Professions*, eds H. Allen and I. Lee, Multicultural Centre, Sydney CAE

Illich, I. 1977, *Disabling Professions*, Marion Boyars, London

Irvine, E. E. 1966, 'A new look at casework', *New Developments in Casework*, ed. E. Younghusband, George Allen & Unwin, London

Ivey, A. E. 1988, *Intentional Interviewing and Counselling*, 2nd edn, Brooks Cole, Pacific Grove

Johnson, L. C. 1989, *Social Work Practice: A Generalist Approach*, Allyn & Bacon, Boston

Kasius, C. ed., 1950, *Principles and Techniques in Social Casework (1940–1950)*, Greenwood Press, Connecticut

Keefe, T. 1980, 'Empathy skill and critical consciousness', *Social Casework*, pp. 387–93

——1984, 'Alienation and social work practice', *Social Casework*, pp. 145–53

Keith-Lucas, A. 1953, 'The political theory implicit in social casework theory', *American Political Science Review*, December, pp. 1076–91

Kellehear, A. 1984, 'Are we a "death-denying" society? A sociological review', *Social Science and Medicine*, vol. 18, no. 9, pp. 713–23

Kellehear, A. and Fook, J. 1989, 'Sociological Factors in Death Denial by the Terminally Ill', *Advances in Behavioural Medicine*, vol. 6, pp. 527–37

Kirk, S. 1983, 'The role of politics in feminist counselling', *Women Changing Therapy,* eds J. H. Robbins and R. J. Siegel, Haworth, New York

Langan, M. and Lee, P. 1989, 'Whatever happened to radical social work', *Radical Social Work Today*, eds M. Langan and P. Lee, Unwin Hyman, London

Laursen, K. 1975, 'Professionalism', *Social Work: Radical Essays*, ed. H. Throssell, University of Queensland Press, St Lucia

Lee, P. 1982, 'Some contemporary and perennial problems of relating theory to practice in social work', *Theory and Practice in Social Work*, eds R. Bailey and P. Lee, Basil Blackwell, Oxford

Leonard, P. 1975, 'Towards a paradigm for radical practice', *Radical Social Work*, eds R. Bailey and M. Brake, Edward Arnold, London

——1984, *Personality and Ideology*, Macmillan, London

Loewenberg, F. M. 1983, *Fundamentals of Social Intervention*, Columbia University Press, New York

London–Edinburgh Weekend Return Group 1980, *In and Against the State*, Pluto Press, London

Longres, J. F. 1981, 'Reactions to working statement on purpose', *Social Work*, pp. 85–7

Longres, J. F. and McLeod, E. 1980, 'Consciousness-raising and social work practice', *Social Casework*, vol. 61, no. 5, pp. 267–76

Lurie, H. L. 1954, 'Responsibilities of a socially oriented profession', *New Directions in Social Work*, ed. C. Kasius, Harper Bros, New York

McHugh, J. 1990, 'Involvement of fathers in child abuse treatment programs', unpublished Bachelor of Social Work Honours Dissertation, Department of Social Work, Monash University, Melbourne

McIntyre, D. 1982, 'On the possibility of "radical" casework: a "radical" dissent', *Contemporary Social Work Education*, vol. 5, no. 3, pp. 191–208

Mailick, M. D. 1977, 'A situational perspective in casework theory', *Social Casework*, vol. 58, no. 7, pp. 401–11

Marchant, H. 1986, 'Gender, systems thinking, and radical social work', *Gender Reclaimed*, eds H. Marchant and B. Wearing, Hale & Iremonger, Sydney, pp. 14–32

Martinez-Brawley, E. E. 1986, 'Beyond cracker-barrel images', *Social Casework*, vol. 67, no. 2, pp. 101–7

Means, R. 1979, 'Which way for "radical" social work?', *British Journal of Social Work*, vol. 9, pp. 15–28

Middleman, R. R. and Goldberg, G. 1974, *Social Service Delivery: A Structural Approach to Social Work Practice*, Columbia University Press, New York

Milford Conference 1974, *Social Casework: Generic and Specific*, American Association of Social Workers, New York

Miller, H. 1968, 'Value dilemmas in social casework', *Social Work*, pp. 27–33

Mills, C. W. 1943, 'The professional ideology of the social pathologist', *American Journal of Sociology*, vol. 49, no. 2, pp. 165–80

——1959, *The Sociological Imagination*, Penguin, Harmondsworth

Moreau, M. J. 1979, 'A structural approach to social work practice', *Canadian Journal of Social Work Education*, vol. 5, no. 1, pp. 78–94

Mowbray, M. 1981, 'A new orthodoxy: all-purpose radicalism', *Australian Social Work*, vol. 34, no. 2, p. 2

Napier, L. and George, J. 1988, 'Social work in health care', *Advances in Social Welfare Education*, eds R. Berreen et al., University of New South Wales, Kensington

Nguyen, C. 1990, 'Barriers to communication between Vietnamese and non-Vietnamese', *Proceedings of the Fifth National Network for Intercultural Communication Conference*, eds J. Fook and C. Rana, La Trobe University, September, pp. 26–31

North, M. 1972, *The Secular Priests*, George Allen & Unwin, London

Northern, H. 1982, *Clinical Social Work*, Columbia University Press, New York

Nursten, J. 1974, *Process of Casework*, Pitman, London

Pearson, G. 1975, *The Deviant Imagination*, Macmillan, London

Pedersen, P. 1987, 'Ten frequent assumptions of cultural bias in counselling', *Network for Intercultural Communication Newsletter*, May, pp. 13–15

Pemberton, A. G. and Locke, R. G. 1971, 'Towards a radical critique of social work and welfare ideology', *Australian Journal of Social Issues*, vol. 35, no. 1, March, pp. 29–35

Perlman, H. H. 1957, *Social Casework: A Problem-solving Process*, University of Chicago Press, Chicago & London

——ed. 1969, *Helping: Charlotte Towle on Social Work and Social Casework*, University of Chicago Press, Chicago & London

——1971a, 'Putting the "Social" Back in Social Casework', *Perspectives on Social Casework*, ed. H. H. Perlman, Temple University Press, Philadelphia

——1971b, 'Social Components of Casework Practice', *Perspectives on Social Casework*, ed. H. H. Perlman, Temple University Press, Philadelphia

Petruchenia, J. 1990, 'Anti-racist welfare practice with immigrants', *Social Change and Social Welfare Practice*, eds J. Petruchenia and R. Thorpe, Hale & Iremonger, Sydney

Pincus, A. and Minahan, A. 1971, *Social Work Practice: Model and Method*, F. E. Peacock, Illinois

Pinderhughes, E B. 1983, 'Empowerment for our clients and for ourselves', *Social Casework*, pp. 331–8

Piven, F. F. and Cloward, R. A. 1971, *Regulating the Poor*, Vintage Books, New York

Plamenatz, J. 1971, *Ideology*, Macmillan, London

Plant, R. 1970, *Social and Moral Theory in Casework*, Routledge & Kegan Paul, London

Pritchard, C. and Taylor, R. 1978, *Social Work: Reform or Revolution?*, Routledge and Kegan Paul, London

Radov, C. G., Masnick, B. R. and Hauser, B. B. 1980, 'Issues in feminist therapy: the work of women's study group', *Alternative Social Services for Women*, ed. N. Gottlieb, Columbia University Press, New York

Reay, R. 1986 'Bridging the gap: a model for integrating theory and practice', *British Journal of Social Work*, vol. 16, pp. 49–64

Rees, S. 1978, *Social Work Face to Face*, Edward Arnold, London

Reid, W. J. and Epstein, I. 1972, *Task-Centred Casework*, Columbia University Press, New York

Rein, M. 1970, 'The crossroads for social work', *Social Work*, vol. 27, no. 2, pp. 18–27

Richmond, M. 1922, *What is Social Casework?*, Russell Sage, New York

Roberts, H. 1981, *Doing Feminist Research*, Routledge & Kegan Paul, London

Roberts, R. and Nee, R. H. 1970, *Theories of Social Casework*. University of Chicago Press, Chicago & London

Robertson, I. 1977, *Sociology*, Worth Publishers, New York

Rojek, C., Peacock, G. and Collins, S. 1988, *Social Work and Received Ideas*, Routledge, London

Rolston, B. and Smyth, M. 1982, 'The spaces between the cases: radical social work in Northern Ireland', *Theory and Practice in Social Work*, eds R. Bailey and P. Lee, Basil Blackwell, Oxford

Rosenfeld, J. M. 1983, 'The domain and expertise of social work: a conceptualisation', *Social Work*, pp. 186–91

Rowbotham, S., Segal, L. and Wainwright, H. 1979, *Beyond the Fragments*, Merlin, London

170   RADICAL CASEWORK

Russianoff, P. 1982, *Why Do I Think I'm Nothing Without a Man?*, Bantam, New York
Ryan, W. 1971, *Blaming the Victim*, Pantheon, New York
Schodek, K. 1981, 'Adjuncts to social casework in the 1980s', *Social Casework*, pp. 195–200
Skenridge, I. and Lennie, P. 1978, 'Social work: the wolf in sheep's clothing', *Arena*, No. 51, pp. 47–92
Simpkin, M. 1979, *Trapped Within Welfare*, 1st edn, Macmillan, London
——1983, *Trapped Within Welfare*, 2nd edn, Macmillan, London
Smid, G. and Van Krieken, R. 1984, 'Notes on theory and practice in social work: a comparative view', *British Journal of Social Work*, vol. 14, pp. 11–22
Soyer, D. 1963, 'The right to fail', *Social Work*, pp. 72–8
Spitzer, K. and Welsh, B. 1979, 'A problem-focused model of practice', *Social Work Processes*, eds B. R. Compton and B. Galaway, Dorsey, Illinois, pp. 257–68
Stanley, L. and Wise, S. 1983, *Breaking Out: Feminist Consciousness and Feminist Research*, Routledge, London
Statham, D. 1978, *Radicals in Social Work*, Routledge & Kegan Paul, London
Steer, M. 1989, 'A powerful concept for disability and service provision', *Australian Social Work*, vol. 42, no. 1, pp. 43–5
Stevenson, O. and Parsloe, P. 1978, *Social Service Teams: the Practitioner's View*, Her Majesty's Stationery Office, London
Stuart, A. 1976, 'Advocacy, judgement and professional social work practice', *Social Work in Australia*, eds P. Boas and J. Crawley, Australian International Press & Publishing, Sydney
Sturdivant, S. 1980, *Therapy With Women*, Springer Publishing Co., New York
Terrell, P. 1973, 'The social worker as radical: roles of advocacy', ed. J. Fischer, *Interpersonal Helping: Emerging Approaches for Social Work Practice*, Charles C. Thomas, Illinois
The Ad Hoc Committee on Advocacy 1969, 'The social worker as advocate: the champion of social victims', *Social Work*, pp. 16–22
Thomas, S. A. 1977, 'Theory and practice in feminist therapy', *Social Work*, pp. 447–54
Thorpe, R. 1981, 'Front line work in state departments of child welfare', unpublished
Thorpe, R. and Petruchenia, J. 1990, 'Introduction', *Social Change and Social Welfare Practice*, eds J. Petruchenia and R. Thorpe, Hale & Iremonger, Sydney
Throssell, H. 1975, 'Social work overview', *Social Work: Radical Essays*, ed. H. Throssell, University of Queensland Press, St Lucia
Tilbury, D.E.F. 1977, *Casework in Context: A Basis for Practice*, Pergamon, Oxford
Tilley, N. 1977, 'No Marx for clients', *Community Care*, 2 March, p. 17
Tomlinson, J. 1977, *Is Band-aid Social Work Enough?*, Wobbly Press, Darwin

Walker, H. and Beaumont, H. 1981, *Probation Work: Critical Theory and Socialist Practice*, Basil Blackwell

Wearing, B. 1984, *The Ideology of Motherhood*, George Allen & Unwin, Sydney

—— 1985, 'Gender and power in social work', *Australian Social Work*, vol. 38, no. 1, pp. 11–18

—— 1986, 'Feminist theory and social work', *Gender Reclaimed*, eds H. Marchant and B. Wearing, Hale & Iremonger, Sydney

Webb, D. 1981, 'Themes and continuities in radical and traditional social work', *British Journal of Social Work*, no. 11, pp. 143–58

—— 1985, 'Social work and critical consciousness: rebuilding orthodoxy', *Issues in Social Work Education*, vol. 5, no. 2, pp. 89–102

Webb, D. and Evans, R. 1978, 'Developing a client-centred sociology', *Community Care*, 22 February, pp. 20–2

Williams, R. A. 1982, 'Client self-determination in social casework: fact or fancy? An exploratory study', *Australian Social Work*, vol. 35, no. 3, pp. 27–34

Wilson, E. 1980, 'Feminism and social work', *Radical Social Work and Practice*, eds R. Bailey and M. Brake, Edward Arnold, London

Wolfensberger, W. 1983, 'Social role valorisation: a proposed new term for the principle of normalisation', *Mental Retardation*, vol. 21, no. 6, pp. 234–9

Wootton, B. 1959, *Social Science and Social Pathology*, George Allen & Unwin, London

Zastrow, C. 1981, *The Practice of Social Work*, Dorsey, Homewood

Index

15, 68; *see also* political, action;
unionising
communication theory, 10
community health centre, 123
community work or action, 32, 40,
74
community resources, 110, 116
conflict analysis, 12
conscientisation *see*
consciousness-raising
consciousness-raising, 14–15, 64,
95, 96–100
conservative social work, 42, 148;
see also casework, traditional
contracts, 103, 105
co-operatives, 111
Corrigan & Leonard, 6, 13, 95
counselling, 24, 26, 53, 77, 149
budget, 27
marriage guidance, 135
crisis intervention, 10, 40, 142
critical
awareness, 115–16; *see also*
consciousness-raising
questioning, 98, 109
theory of society, 29
cultural
background, 21
differences, 68
influences, 89
groups, 111
culture 60, 71, 76, 151
non-Western, 59–62
traditional, 150
Western, 59, 62, 151

de-institutionalisation, 112, 147
democracy, 29
denial of death, 76–8
dependency, 110, 120
dependent behaviour, 85
depressed people, 100, 112, 137
depression, 34, 75, 79–80, 87, 133
determinist model, 30
deviance, 3, 11, 62, 78
deviant group, 25–6, 64, 68
dialogical relationship, 104
direct social work, 1, 12, 23
disabilities, 1, 64, 65, 76–9, 82,

87–8, 111, 114, 117, 119, 124,
144
developmental, 93, 110, 135, 137
intellectual, 117, 120
disadvantage, 149
disadvantaged background, 124
disadvantaged groups, 13, 62–3
disaster, 150
discourse theory, 16, 17
divorcees, 81
dominance, 68

eclectic approach, 9
ecological approach, 13, 39
education, 96, 99, 107–9; *see also*
tertiary education
Egan, 112–13
elderly, the, 149
empathy, 52–3, 109, 112, 152
definition of, 112
empowerment, 17, 88, 102–3
environmental change, 25; *see also*
social change
methods, 22, 23
epilepsy, 118
equality, 105, 143
ethics, 31
objectivity, 61
of individualisation, 27, 61
of respect, 61
self-determination, 12, 30, 31,
61, 144–5, 151
ethical issues, 2
ethnic minority, 62
ethnicity *see* culture; cultural
background
existential approaches *see*
humanistic approaches

family therapy, 10
father
role of, 71, 79
feminine characteristics, 62, 85
feminism
and rural dwellers, 150
and work with men, 149
feminist
analysis, 2, 14, 70
critique of professions, 61–2

pensioner, 94, 109
  aged, 80
Perlman, 20, 28
'person in situation', 20
'personal is political, 15
personal liberation, 9
Petruchenia, 17
policy, 92, 94
political
  action, 32, 68, 103; see also
    collective work or action;
    unionising
  parties, 6
post-modern social work, 5
post-structural perspectives, 16, 17
poverty, 25–7, 81
  culture of, 58
powerlessness see alienation
praxis, 15, 39, 108
professional
  accountability, 11, 83
  distancing, 11, 60, 104
professionalism 9
psychiatrist, 129, 131, 136
psychoanalytic theory, 30
psychodynamic model, 9, 10, 23, 76–7
psychological
  aspects of problems, 43, 75, 104
  methods, 13, 22, 23, 40, 43
  needs, 98
  techniques, 24, 110
psychologist, 128, 129, 135–6, 139
psychology, 40
psychotherapy/psychotherapeutic
  techniques, 23–4, 96
public welfare, 146

racial minorities, 149
racism, 124–5
radical
  debate, 1, 2
  liberal, 31
  Marxist, 31
  'non-intervention', 12
  social work, definition of, 7–9
    in Australia, 17, 68
referral, 92, 105
reframing, 86
relationship between

individual and society, 20–2, 24
  personal and social, 32
religion, 106
research, 24, 92, 152
revolution, 31
right to disagree, 145
role
  change, 84–5
  conflict, 84, 119
  theory, 10
'role distancing', 76
rural
  areas, 105, 133
  disadvantage, 133
  dwellers, 149, 150
  life, 128
  town, 131, 140
  village, 127

schizophrenia, 82, 89
school refusal, 45, 86
secondary gain, 85
self
  awareness, 156–60
  defeating beliefs, 58, 80, 86–8
  determination see ethics
  disclosure, 104, 137
  help, 61
semi-professions, 61
sexist attitudes, 148
sexual
  promiscuity, 123, 127
  safety, 120
  violence, 124
sheltered
  employment, 123
  workshop, 93, 118
Simpkin, 14, 31, 93
social
  change, 6, 7, 9, 12, 15, 17, 21,
    25–6, 30–1, 33, 68
    personal problems in, 82
  sanctions, 81
  class see class
  conformity, 62, 66, 71
  context, 20
  control, 6–8, 28–9, 32, 33
    definition of, 60
    sanctions, 81